ARCTIC

FOREST

NORTHEAST
WOODLANDS

GREAT LAKES

NORTH
ATLANTIC
COAST

AMERICAN

PRAIRIE

APPALACHIAN
HIGHLANDS

SOUTH
ATLANTIC
COAST
AND
PIEDMONT

SOUTHERN
HILL
COUNTRY

GULF COAST

Stories from Where We Live

The California Coast

The *Stories from Where We Live* Series

Each volume in the *Stories from Where We Live* series celebrates a North American ecoregion through its own distinctive literature. For thousands of years, people have told stories to convey their community's cultural and natural history. *Stories from Where We Live* reinvigorates that tradition in hopes of helping young people better understand the place where they live. The anthologies feature poems, stories, and essays from historical and contemporary authors, as well as from the oral traditions of each region's indigenous peoples. Together they document the geographic richness of the continent and reflect the myriad ways that people interact with and respond to the natural world. We hope that these stories kindle readers' imaginations and inspire them to explore, observe, ponder, and protect the place they call home.

Please visit www.worldashome.org for a teaching guide to this book and more information on the *Stories from Where We Live* series.

Stories from Where We Live

The California Coast

EDITED BY SARA ST. ANTOINE

Maps by Paul Mirocha
Illustrations by Trudy Nicholson

MILKWEED EDITIONS

Published 2001 by Milkweed Editions
Printed in Canada
Jacket design by Paul Mirocha
Jacket and interior illustrations by Trudy Nicholson
Jacket and interior maps by Paul Mirocha
Interior design by Wendy Holdman
The text of this book is set in Legacy.
01 02 03 04 05   5 4 3 2 1
First Edition

Milkweed Editions, a nonprofit publisher, gratefully acknowledges support from World
As Home funder, the Lila Wallace-Reader's Digest Fund, as well as operating support from
the Elmer L. and Eleanor J. Andersen Foundation; Bush Foundation; Faegre and Benson
Foundation; General Mills Foundation; Marshall Field's Project Imagine with support from
the Target Foundation and Target Stores; McKnight Foundation; Minnesota State Arts
Board through an appropriation by the Minnesota State Legislature and a grant from
the National Endowment for the Arts; Norwest Foundation on behalf of Norwest Bank
Minnesota; Lawrence and Elizabeth Ann O'Shaughnessy Charitable Income Trust in honor
of Lawrence M. O'Shaughnessy; Oswald Family Foundation; Ritz Foundation on behalf
of Mr. and Mrs. E. J. Phelps Jr.; John and Beverly Rollwagen Fund of the Minneapolis
Foundation; St. Paul Companies, Inc.; U.S. Bancorp Foundation; and generous individuals.

Library of Congress Cataloging-in-Publication Data

Stories from where we live. The California coast / edited by Sara St. Antoine.
    p.   cm. — (Stories from where we live)
ISBN 1-57131-631-0 (cloth)
    1. Pacific Coast (Calif.)—Miscellanea—Juvenile literature. 2. Pacific Coast
(Calif.)—Biography—Juvenile literature. 3. Natural history—California—Pacific
Coast—Miscellanea—Juvenile literature. 4. Pacific Coast (Calif.)—Literary collections.
5. American literature—California—Pacific Coast. [1. Pacific Coast (Calif.)—Literary
collections.] I. Title: California coast. II. St. Antoine, Sara, 1966–   III. Series.

F868.P33 C34 2001
979.4'00946—dc21
                                                                    2001018326

Stories from Where We Live
The California Coast

Great Places

Reapers and Sowers

Wild Lives

Appendixes: Ecology of the California Coast

An Invitation

In the mid-nineteenth century, people living in the eastern United States frequently encountered printed notices describing the splendors of California and inviting them to book passage on the next ship bound for its shore.

In a similar spirit, this book is our invitation to you to discover the riches of the California Coast—whether you live in the region or far away. We don't have seats to offer on any ship, of course. Instead, we offer you stories about sea otters and salt marshes, essays about surfers and treefrogs, and poems about plum trees and poppies. With these writings, new and old, you'll journey through the California Coast region and meet some of its distinctive people, plants, and animals.

The California Coast ecoregion as we define it stretches from the California-Oregon border south to the tip of the Baja Peninsula. This entire area is influenced by the presence of the Pacific Ocean and by a mild Mediterranean climate. But if you were to hike its full length you'd pass through a variety of natural settings: fern-filled redwood forests, coastal mountains, rocky shores and sea cliffs, salt marshes, lakes, chaparral-covered hillsides, and coastal scrublands. You'd also pass through hundreds of human communities—including the cities of San Francisco and Los Angeles—and see the way people have shaped these wild lands into farms, ranches, neighborhoods, roadways, parks, and downtowns.

For nearly ten thousand years, this region was home to the Luiseño, the Chumash, the Ohlone, and dozens of other native groups. Some of their stories persist even to the present day, giving us a glimpse of their lives and the natural world that sustained them. But these aren't the only stories rooted in the California Coast. As each new set of inhabitants migrated to the region, they too articulated their experiences and thoughts in oral and written narratives. In this way, the stories, poems, songs, journals, and essays of the California Coast are a vibrant record of the region's cultural and natural heritage.

This anthology represents just a bit of this rich literary tradition. As you'll see, we've divided the anthology into four parts. "Adventures" recounts some action-filled moments in the region—from the exuberant to the terrifying. "Great Places" celebrates a number of favorite natural areas. "Reapers and Sowers" chronicles some of the diverse ways that people have harvested from and tended this coastal region over time. And "Wild Lives" brings you closer to some of the region's leafy, prickly, furry, finned, and feathered living things.

We hope this collection enriches your understanding of the California Coast. And we hope it inspires you to take a bold and marvelous journey to the place where you live.

—Sara St. Antoine

Stories from Where We Live

The California Coast

Adventures

Almost a Hanging

GRETCHEN WOELFLE

To Madeline and Ran Erskine

Between 1848 and the early 1860s, California was buzzing with the exploits and excitement of the Gold Rush. "Gold fever" made every day an adventure whether there was gold in one's pan or not.

Young George Erskine worked at a shipyard in Thomaston, Maine, hewing giant logs into spars and ribs for schooners and clipper ships that sailed all around the world. One day a sailing ship brought his cousin Abial home from the California Gold Rush.

"I didn't make a fortune," Abial admitted, "but I climbed mountains so high there was hardly enough air to fill my lungs. I saw a desert so dry that nothing lived there but ornery cactus and ugly lizards."

George had never seen mountains or desert or cactus.

"I saw Indians, mountain men, and prospectors so rough you get splinters on your eyelids just looking at them. It seems half the world is moving to California. Some folks find gold. All of them find adventure."

George wanted adventure. "I'll try my luck," he said. So he packed up his tools and, just after his seventeenth birthday, he sailed for California.

In San Francisco George bought a mining pan and a red flannel shirt, and caught a boat up the Sacramento River. At Sacramento he bought a mule and headed north to Middle Creek. Rushing streams tumbled down mountainsides covered with ponderosa pines. Patches of brown canvas marked the mining camps. Most miners lived in canvas tents. After working twelve hours a day, they had no time left to make life comfortable.

For weeks George trudged up one mountain and down another. Day after day he filled a pan with gravel and water from a stream. He swirled the pan, washing away the gravel. Heavy gold flakes—if there were any—sank to the bottom. But George found barely enough gold to buy the food he needed to stay alive. It wasn't easy when one egg cost three dollars!

Thousands of men roamed the California hills hoping to get rich. Some didn't know a hammer from a handsaw. But George knew, so he unpacked his toolbox. He got jobs cutting posts for mine props and logs for dams. He built square wooden pipes and sluice boxes too. Miners made dams to channel water through pipes and sluices set in the stream. The long sluice boxes had ribs, or riffle bars, nailed along the bottom. Miners shoveled mud into them and the flowing water washed away dirt and sand. Heavier gold dust sank and got caught in the riffle bars.

Soon George was making more money than most prospectors. All went well for him until one night when darkness black as river mud covered the camp.

"Erskine! George Erskine! Where are you? We'll find you, so you'd better show your face!"

"Quit hollerin'!" called a groggy voice from the nearby tents. "Erskine's over by the big pine tree."

George crawled out of his tent and met a rifle, inches from his nose. At the end of the rifle stood Mort, a skinny man with a grizzled gray beard.

"Here he is," Red shouted, waving a lantern at George.

"Here I am," George echoed. "What's going on?" He slowly lifted his eyes from the rifle to the lantern. In the flickering light George saw Red's bushy black hair and pasty white face.

Mort nudged the rifle barrel toward George. "You the one who built us them pipes and sluices, right?"

"A-yuh," said George in his Maine way. His voice sounded shaky. He took a deep breath.

"Out West you don't cheat your customers," a voice growled from the shadows.

"That you, Fritz?" George called, trying to sound friendly. Fritz ignored his greeting.

"As soon as you left, those sluice boxes stopped working," said Mort.

"So we plan to string you from the nearest tree," muttered Fritz, who was tying a noose in the end of a rope.

George froze. He'd heard of vigilante gangs killing men for less than a broken sluice box. Frontier justice is what they called it.

"I stand by my work," George said in a steady voice, but not feeling too steady inside. "I built those boxes out of prime timber."

"All I know is they don't work," Red shouted.

Maybe he got his name from his red-hot temper, George thought. Better not show him I'm scared.

"Did the boxes come loose?" George asked.

"No, they're just like you left 'em. But the water don't drain out and we can't get our gold if it don't," said Fritz. "We already lost a day's work."

"I'll look at them as soon as it gets light," George offered. "And I'll fix them. No charge."

"You won't live that long," growled Mort.

"Tonight then. I'll look at them right now," George replied. "I'm not a crook." When he talked tough, he felt braver.

"Well," allowed Red, "there are trees at our camp we can hang you from."

George trudged upstream with wet boots, a rifle at his back, and three men who wanted to hang him for an outlaw! Why, they were no better than outlaws themselves! He'd stand his ground. He didn't come all the way to California to get hanged!

When they finally got to the men's camp, George stood in freezing water up to his knees and inspected his work. It was getting light now.

A square wooden pipe carried stream water to the sluice box. The water should have run through the sluice and back into the stream. Sure enough, water was going into the pipe, but none was coming out the other end. George held the lantern close to it. He checked the joints, looking for faults and leaks. Everything was snug and tight.

"The pipe isn't leaking," said George.

"So what?" said Fritz. "It don't work."

"I'll pry off the top." George pulled and strained and the board popped off. Water hit him in the face. He felt around the pipe and something slapped him.

He jumped back. "What's that?" He groped with two hands and pulled out a huge flapping salmon.

"There's your problem," George cried. "A salmon swam into the pipe and got wedged in tight."

The men stared at the salmon, then at George, then at each other. Red chuckled, then Fritz. Soon the whole bunch was laughing, even George.

Suddenly the salmon shot out of George's hands and landed on the bank. It wiggled on the sand, trying to reach the water. Mort dove for the fish and tripped Red who fell on top of Fritz. Mort tried to stand, but fell down again as George lunged beneath him for the salmon.

The four of them flipped and flopped on the ground, laughing and shouting and grabbing for the fish. When they finally picked themselves up, George held tight to the salmon.

"Let's try the culprit," Mort cried.

"Guilty on account of he plugged up the pipe," Fritz called out.

"I sentence him to death by frying!" Red added.

"That's better than a hanging," George allowed. "Let's eat!"

Gretchen Woelfle *lives in Venice, California, and writes stories and environmental nonfiction for children. This story is based on a true incident in the life of George B. Erskine (1838–1929), who was born in Palermo, Maine. George made two trips out West during the gold and silver rush of the 1850s and 1860s. Then he returned to Maine where he bought a farm, married, and raised five sons.*

The Real Work

GARY SNYDER

(Today with Zach & Dan rowing by Alcatraz
and around Angel Island)

sea-lions and birds,
sun through fog
flaps up and lolling,
looks you dead in the eye.
sun haze;
a long tanker riding light and high.

sharp wave choppy line—
interface tide-flows—
seagulls sit on the meeting
eating;
we slide by white-stained cliffs.

the real work.
washing and sighing,
sliding by.

Gary Snyder *has authored many collections of nature poetry and essays. He teaches courses in literature and wilderness thought at the University of California at Davis and lives in the foothills of the Sierras.*

The Long Bike Ride

MÉLINA BROWN

California's rocky shores are an ideal place to watch the surf crash, clamber over rocks, and go exploring. And sometimes that's just the beginning of the day's adventure.

"Look out for the rock!" Jake yelled at me. I turned away from Michael to look straight ahead, but I didn't see any rock.

"Made you look," laughed Jake, speeding up to pass me.

Jake Hernandez and Michael Choi were my two best friends. I biked with them whenever I could because Mama didn't like me biking on my own, and I sure wasn't about to go with my little sister, Keyana. Keyana had to stay in her after-school program anyway.

Dad had said I was supposed to stay away from certain areas of the old army base, Fort Ord. Unexploded grenades had been buried there, and lead bullets still littered the dunes near old target ranges. He hadn't told me to stay away from the other side of Highway 1, though, probably because he never thought I'd go there. He knows I don't like the water. It's freezing, even in summer.

I had learned about that the hard way. When Michael and Jake first brought me to the beach, I had taken off my T-shirt and run right into the water with nothing on but my swimming trunks. Cold shocked through my body like lightning and I jumped right out. When I ran back, shivering and shouting, both Jake and Michael were doubled over in laughter. "Antoine, man! I can't believe you did that!" laughed Jake as he zipped up a black rubber outfit.

"Hey, Antoine, we forgot to tell you. You need a wet suit around here," Michael had added with concern, before breaking out in laughter again. Since then, I'd begged Mama and Dad for one, but Dad said I was lucky I got a mountain bike for my fourteenth birthday. I'd have to get a job and start saving for anything else I wanted.

I tightened my helmet as we bounced over sandy bumps and jumped over mounded cypress tree roots. Cypress trees are so different from the evergreens I saw near the army base in Georgia, where Dad was stationed before being transferred out here. Their branches spread out with flat bunches of needles, like they're trying to reach the water.

We rode down a trail, past the dunes, avoiding the thorny shrubs and tufts of needlegrass. In science, we'd learned how to identify these and other beach plants that grow in the dunes. We also learned that we had to be careful and ride on the packed, wet sand so we didn't contribute to beach erosion.

We followed the wet part of the beach as it curved around in wavy arcs. The sky had been steel gray all day, but I didn't care. It felt good to be riding next to the ocean, with wind whipping my face and cold sprinkles of water splashing up from the waves washing ashore. Even though I had just turned fourteen, I felt like a man. I didn't have to worry about all my parents' rules out here. I was free.

We pedaled for a long time, racing then coasting, until the

beach became rocky. Waves crashed against rocky little ridges, sending showers of water into the air.

"Hey, guys, we're almost at the Aquarium." Jake pointed straight ahead. "I think we've gone at least six miles."

"Yeah, and I think it's time for a break," Michael said, jumping off his bike and landing in the sand. Jake joined him, but I rode a little farther toward the rocks.

"What's the matter? You guys can't go the distance, hmmm?" I said, teasing them. I threw my arms in the air over my head as if I'd just won a race. "Antoine Graves wins his *third* triathlon! Antoine, how *do* you do it?" I said in a loud sports announcer's voice. Maybe Michael and Jake were good swimmers, but no one could outdistance me on a bike.

Michael shook his head at me then lay down on the sand. Jake said, "Show-off. We'll see how far you ride when you wreck your new bike!" Then he lay down too.

I pedaled until the sand ended. The black cluster of rocks stopped me, blocking my way like a small mountain. I got off my bike and just stood there, a few feet from the waves. I still didn't like the water, but I sure didn't mind being near it. From a distance, the water looked as dark as the steel gray sky. But at my feet, it was so clear I could see the red and peach-colored starfish stretching on the rocks like sunbathers. They looked soft and furry, like velvet. I almost expected them to stand up and start swaying with the waves, dancing to the music of the ocean.

The mist sprinkled and cooled me down from the ride. But when it really started to chill me, I turned around to head back. Then I heard a loud cry. It could not have come from the black cormorants flapping above me. A chill ran down my spine. What was it?

I inched my bike closer to the rocks and closer to the harsh, hoarse cry. If I had been younger and still believed in monsters, I would have guessed it was an evil sea creature. But the more I listened to it, the more it actually sounded like a moaning, yelping cry for help. It sounded like something being tortured. I had to see what it was.

I climbed up onto the slippery rock, using my hands the way I'd seen rock climbers do. The water gurgled and chugged as it splashed into the narrow passages between each rock. I climbed over a few more rocks, peeking down into each cranny. Then I saw the sea creature down in a crevice in the rocks. It wasn't an evil one, though. It stared at me with big, sad, filmy eyes. It was a sea lion pup and it was stuck.

I leaned on the closest rock, trying to avoid the slimy sea-weed and curly barnacles coating the sides of it. I reached over and stuck my hand out to pet the sea lion. Luckily, I was still out of reach because the sea lion flashed its sharp teeth and tried to bite me! But only its long, stiff whiskers scraped my hand. They looked like porcupine quills and felt like them too. I looked at the whisker marks on my hand, wondering what would have happened if its teeth had made contact instead.

I backed away and watched as the sea lion's nostrils flared up and then closed to let out another wail. Its mouth was like a pink cavern, letting out so much sound I thought people back in Seaside would be able to hear it. But the waves crashed harder against the rocks, drowning out even those scared moans.

I looked more closely at the sea lion, trying to see if it was cut or hurt. Its coat looked dark and oily, the same color as the rocks. Its front flippers perched on a rock, but I couldn't see its hind flippers. They must have been wedged in between the rocks. How would it ever get out?

"Hey, Antoine!" came Michael's voice from behind me. "We couldn't see you anymore. We thought you'd fallen in or something. What are you doing?"

Before I could answer, Jake's voice jumped in. "Wow! It's a seal. You trying to talk to it or something?" he laughed.

"It's a sea lion," I answered, pointing to its tiny ears, which stuck out like little flaps. I'd learned that seals didn't have them. "It's stuck." The sea lion opened its mouth again to holler, and Jake and Michael laughed at the sound.

"Let's try to free it," said Michael, reaching toward the sea lion.

"No!" I yelled as he extended his arm. "It'll try to bite you!"

The sea lion lunged at Michael's hand before I had even finished my sentence. Michael pulled back his hand quicker than I had. He didn't even get nicked by the sea lion's whiskers.

"Whoa!" Jake laughed from a safe distance. "That little guy is fierce!"

Michael jumped off the rock and immediately started scanning the nearby sand. He stooped to pick up a long branch, then ran back. "We'll use this," he said with a smile.

He inched closer to the sea lion again, and I couldn't help feeling annoyed. The sea lion was my discovery, and now Michael was going to poke it with a stick.

"Leave it alone, Michael," I ordered. "It didn't do anything to you."

"Just relax, Antoine. I'm trying to help free it. Maybe I can just push it out with this branch."

"Stop!" I yelled as Michael moved to poke the sea lion. "That's not going to help it. Just put the branch down." The sea lion yelped even more when a loud clap of thunder burst nearby.

"We should get out of here, guys," Jake said, inching himself off the rocks. "Look at the sky!" He pointed to the black clouds hovering over us.

Michael threw the branch into the water and shook his head. "That thing won't budge. It's really stuck. Man, and now it's going to storm on us!" He ran to his bike as if he'd completely forgotten about the stranded sea lion.

I stared at the pup again, then at the sky. It would take us awhile to get back and I'd be in serious trouble if I were caught this far away from home. But I didn't want to leave the sea lion alone. What would happen to it?

"Come on, Antoine!" Jake yelled back at me. They were already pedaling away. Fat raindrops started pelting me. I had to go. I took one last look at the sea lion, then got on my bike and rode away.

"You're in *big* trouble, Antoine! Dad said you should've been back by five o'clock." Keyana looked up at me with wide, worried eyes.

I brushed past her and glanced at the kitchen clock. Six-thirty. Mama worked at the hospital until eight o'clock on Thursdays. I'd have to face Dad alone. What would I tell him? Would he understand if I told him about the sea lion? He called me before I had a chance to decide. I grabbed a kitchen towel to dry myself, but I was soaking wet.

"Look at the time, Antoine. What have you been doing?" Dad tapped his watch so hard he could have broken it. He had changed out of his uniform, but he still wore his serious face.

"Dad, I didn't mean to be late. I was just biking around and we lost track of time—and—"

"Who's 'we'?"

"Jake and Michael and me. I didn't realize it had gotten so late because we were—"

"The same guys who let you jump into freezing water? What were you guys up to?" Dad's eyes were on fire.

"We were just biking and stuff and—"

"Just biking? All this time? I don't want to hear any more excuses right now. Go eat the stir-fry I saved for you before your mother gets back. If you hurry, you should have time to do the dishes and your homework by then, too. We'll have to see how she feels about grounding you."

I slunk back into the kitchen, knowing better than to argue anymore with Dad. I scowled at Keyana from her peeking spot on the upstairs landing. It wasn't fair—getting in trouble for trying to save a sea lion. Why couldn't Dad understand? I hadn't done anything wrong. Who would save the sea lion now? And what if Jake or Michael went back before me?

All night I thought about how I could get back to that spot. Mom and Dad still hadn't listened to my story and had grounded me from using the phone, but not from using my bike. They knew it was the quickest way for me to get to school. And that's how I'd get back to the beach. I'd bike back the next day, alone.

When Dad's heavy knock on my door woke me up the next morning, all I could think about was how much I wanted to keep sleeping. Then I remembered the sea lion and my plan to save it. I sprang out of bed and quickly got ready for school.

When I got to the kitchen, Mama's face reminded me that I was still in trouble. She looked at me with disappointment in her eyes as she went to do Keyana's hair. That's when I slowed down. What had I been thinking? I didn't want them mad at me anymore. The plan I'd thought up was crazy. I couldn't risk getting in trouble again like I had the day before. But why hadn't they let me explain?

I started feeling angry and scraped the chair loudly as I pulled it away from the table. Dad stared at me over his newspaper with his 'don't-start-with-me' look. I tried not to look his way as I sat down to eat my cereal, but a headline caught my attention.

"What's wrong now?" Dad confronted me as I stared his way.

I tilted my head to read the article from Dad's lowered paper.

Sea Lion Escapes!

A sea lion pup caught in a crevice swam away shortly after Aquarium workers arrived. They'd received numerous phone calls from beachcombers about the young sea lion, which had been spotted as early as Tuesday. When workers arrived, however, the sea lion just swam away. "It had probably lost weight, being stuck there for a few days," commented one of the Aquarium outreach employees. . . .

"That's the sea lion I found yesterday!" I blurted out.

Dad squinted at me, waiting for an explanation. Before I could stop myself, words flowed out of me like rain from the night before. "I found the stranded sea lion and I wanted to free him and then it looked like a storm was coming and—"

"When did all this happen?" Dad looked at me hard.

"When we were biking," I said, moving my eyes back down to the article.

Dad looked at me as if he were putting together a puzzle. After several minutes, he said quietly, "Well, I'm glad to know you don't hate being near the water anymore." He shook his head in disbelief. "My son, Antoine Graves, rescuer of sea lions," he chuckled.

"But I didn't save it. I wanted to. I wish I had been the one to do it." Then I wondered what would have happened if I had been able to touch it, feed it, or move it. Would I have helped?

I looked back at the article, relieved that the sea lion had escaped and that I didn't have to execute my plan. When I looked up, I caught Dad smiling at me, the way he does when he's with his friends. I don't think he saw a know-nothing little boy anymore. He looked the way I'd always wanted him to be: proud.

Mélina Brown *was born in France, raised in Michigan, Wisconsin, and Minnesota, and reincarnated in North Carolina. She attended the College of St. Thomas, the Sorbonne, and the University of North Carolina at Chapel Hill. Ms. Brown works as a school librarian. Her writing has appeared in* Library Talk *and* Life Notes: Personal Writings by Contemporary Black Women *(W. W. Norton), as well as in literary journals and on public radio. She is completing her third novel for young people.*

Quicksand on the Gaviota Coast

J. Smeaton Chase

In 1911, J. Smeaton Chase and his horse, Chino, journeyed up the rough roads and beach trails of the Pacific coast from Mexico to Oregon. In this account, Chase describes a perilous passage along the Gaviota coast, south of Point Conception.

The country hereabout is monotonous and unattractive. Low undulating hills run for mile on mile, treeless, and scanty even of brush, and the cañons are dry and shadeless. We marched some miles before finding water, and I resolved to camp at the first creek I should see. At last I came to one, which afforded good pasturage also; and, dismounting, I led Chino down toward the beach, where I noticed a little bench of green grass at the mouth of the cañon and on the very edge of the shore sand.

Here the expedition narrowly escaped disaster. The inwash of the tide, meeting the water of the creek, had formed an area, a sort of pit, of quicksand. This we had to cross in order to reach the beach, and in a moment, without warning, I was up to my middle, and Chino, following close behind, plunged in beside and almost upon me. On the instant I threw myself backward, and tried to work myself out, but the sand clogged me as if it were liquid lead, and I could not reach back with my hands to where the solid ground would give me support. Chino, meanwhile, was struggling desperately but helplessly, the heavy saddle-bags and other articles of his load weighing him down so that he was already half covered.

By great good fortune the cañon wall was nearby, not over eight feet away. It was of weathered rock, soft and shaley, and I thought that if I could anyhow work over to it I could get grip enough on it to support myself. It seemed an impossible thing to do, with the fatal sand clasping and weighing me down, but I attempted it.

I remember that, as I struggled, a horror of the commonplace sunlit evening flashed over me and, with it, the thought that no one would ever know what had happened to me, for there would be no trace, no clue. That horrible sand would close over me, the sun would shine on the spot, the roar of waves would go on unbroken; I should simply cease to be. I think I wondered whether there would not be any way of telling my friends; but I am not sure whether that thought came then, or in thinking it over afterward.

All this can only have taken a very short time, during which I was struggling to reach the rocky wall. At last my fingers scraped the rock, and gradually I was able to draw myself backward to firm ground. Then I ran round by the solid beach sand, crossing the creek, and came back to Chino. He had stopped struggling, but lay over on his side, and had sunk so that one of the saddle-bags was quite out of sight. Blood, too, was spattered all about him.

Coming as close as was safe behind him, I gradually loosened as much of his load as I could reach. Then I caught his rope and tried to get him to exert himself. For some time he made no move, and I thought he must have broken his off-side foreleg on a half-buried snag of dead wood that projected above the sand. Again and again I tried to get him to move, but he still lay on his side, drawing great gasping breaths, and I about decided I should have to shoot him where he lay. But I made a last effort, shouting and hauling at him with all my strength, until I literally forced him to bestir himself: when, putting my last ounce into it, I pulled and shouted, refusing to allow him to relax his efforts for a moment and gradually working his head round somewhat toward where I stood. With a final wild spasm he scrambled up onto the dry, hard sand and stood snorting and trembling pitifully, bespattered with blood and utterly exhausted.

I was vastly relieved to find that the blood was coming from his mouth and nostrils. He had broken some small blood vessel in his first struggles. I took off the saddle and led him carefully over to a grassy spot, where I washed out his mouth and then gave him a thorough rubbing down; and within half an hour I had the satisfaction of seeing my staunch companion of so many days and nights feeding with equanimity and even enthusiasm.

The incident was sufficiently dangerous to give me a lesson in caution, as well as cause for hearty thankfulness. There was not the slightest hint of treachery in the appearance of the sand, but thereafter I went warily in all doubtful places. I ransacked my rescued saddle-bags and made a rare supper to celebrate the adventure. As the bags were strongly made, and waterproofed, the contents had not been much damaged. Then I ran up my sleeping tent, in view of the fog which I could see advancing from the sea. I chose a place on a little shelf of dry sand, sheltered by the angle of the cañon wall, and apparently above high-water mark by a safe though narrow margin. Then in the dusk I gathered a pile of driftwood and made a royal fire, by which I sat until long after dark, listening with more than usual enjoyment to the tinkle of Chino's bell and the manifold voices of the sea.

J. Smeaton Chase *was born in England in 1864 and emigrated to Los Angeles in 1890. He wrote six books about the natural wonders of California, including* California Coast Trails, *from which this account is drawn. He died in 1923.*

Napa during El Niño

CHRISTINA HUTCHINS

You are not the center of the world.

But at the bend in the river
all the floodwaters
urge slide turn
directly toward me
on the bank
unbury their muscled force
at my feet

and beyond
they furl away and away
from me
on downriver
mad brown rush
with still so much to follow

I am before
the waters
and behind them

Christina Hutchins *spends most days in Berkeley, California, where she teaches at the Pacific School of Religion. Her poems have appeared in many literary journals and anthologies, and in a chapbook and compact disc,* Collecting Light *(Acacia Books, 1999). Born in San Jose before it became Silicon Valley, she has wandered the California Coast for enough years to carry the place in her bones. And still it surprises her.*

Surfing with Sharks

DANIEL DUANE

Many sharks dwell in the waters off the California Coast. Most species are harmless, and the chances of being attacked by the remaining varieties are extraordinarily small. But as Daniel Duane conveys in this excerpt from his book Caught Inside, *surfers have special reason to be concerned. They spend hours on the water, and when they lie on their boards they're thought to resemble seals and sea lions—favorite foods of great whites and other big sharks.*

An idle surfer has plenty to think about, like sharks: naturally, one takes an interest in them, studies photographs of their gaping, bloody mouths—prostrate on the decks of fishing boats or on municipal piers, great whites always seem a ghastly and naked smear of triangular teeth and pale, fleshy gums. And when stared at all afternoon, the stuffed great white at the San Francisco Aquarium—thirteen feet long and somewhat deflated in its freezer case—serves reasonably well as an embodiment of one's relationship to fate: you know they're out there, you even know they're more likely to be at one place than another, and, yet, the odds are on your side. You either quit surfing (unthinkable), or accept a sentiment commonly shared in the water: "Yeah, I figure, if a shark's going to eat me, he's going to eat me." Sensible enough, although one feels compelled to ask how many aspects of late-twentieth-century American life involve the possibility of being devoured by a two-thousand-pound predator with razor teeth. A kid I knew in high school had once seen coroner's photographs of a Monterey surfer bitten almost in half—he repeatedly told me how most of the man's rib cage was gone and how his organs spilled across the table. The board had beached first, with a classic cookie-cutter bite missing; the body drifted in the cold currents for nearly two weeks before it was found. Years later, another local man was having a great time at a remote reef when he felt as if someone had dropped a VW on his back— suddenly he was underwater facing a huge eye. And in Oregon, a shark bit the board out from under a surfer who was sitting in wait for a wave; that awful mouth surged up and chomped onto the fiberglass between his legs. The shark bolted with the board in its teeth, dragging the surfer along by the ankle leash; when the shark turned to charge, the surfer grabbed its tail— two other surfers witnessed this—and they wheeled around in circles together before it let go.

There were whole weeks that fall when the Point was no good. . . . Somehow Vince and his friend, whose name was Willie Gonzales, were never even checking it on those days, having apparently predicted its conditions through remote observations. But that's one of the sport's mysteries: one must be available, flexible, always in shape. A storm could break for one day and produce the greatest four hours your reef has seen in a decade, only to pick up the next and blow the waves apart. One comes to welcome serendipity into the patterns of daily life, accept the fleeting nature of happiness, and avoid all unnecessary time constraints. But even when I could find waves, the cold occasionally felt like a kind of oppressive duty;

sometimes I wanted to just hide indoors, drink some hot tea. On one such stormy afternoon, I took coffee and a big Toll House cookie (my unqualified favorite food) over to the Santa Cruz Surf Museum at the lighthouse for a look at the obligatory chewed-up board. A small room with the air of a temple, the museum had a historical range of boards hung all over the walls, from redwood planks to the latest big-wave elephant guns. Old black-and-white photographs showed smiling boys in simpler times; an older gentleman wearing a satin Santa Cruz Longboarders Association jacket mentioned that the winter of '41 was a beaut. And then I found it: huge teeth had crunched the fiberglass like a potato chip, tangible evidence of a phantom reaper, like the footprints of a yeti or film footage of a ghost. A glass case held photographs of Erik Larsen, the victim, in bed, with heavily bandaged arms; handwritten doctor's reports described deep lacerations and massive blood loss. Pieces of wetsuit, also behind glass, looked as if they'd been shredded by a tree mulcher. A photo caption compared territorial bites to feeding bites, said Larsen was slated for dinner. Expecting fatty seal meat instead of fiberglass and neoprene, lean muscle and bone, sharks usually spit surfers out; but the one that got Larsen had come back for a second bite.

Still, tide dropping, big storm on the way and time wasting, I said my mantras—"more likely to be killed by a drunk driver, more likely to be struck by lightning"—and drove north. All the way up the coast, I felt the dread of true wilderness, of getting an upward view in the food chain—something humans have worked hard at avoiding. . . . I changed into my wetsuit with a little reggae on the tape deck. . . . On the path, panicked cottontails scampered into the dead hemlock as I passed. I paddled out in water slate-gray and disappointingly flat, caught a little nothing of an ankle-high wave, then drifted about and took comfort in the water's murkiness—concentrated on surfaces, ignored the way my legs faded down into the milky green. Smelled the brine, watched granite-colored light wave along the still outer waters. There's a rare quality of sun and shade here on cloudy days, with the dramatic contrasts of black-and-white film. Sunbeams hit a patch of outer sea with glaring intensity, the water so bright against the black distance as to appear shivering and splashing in response to the light. Vince was nowhere to be seen, hadn't been for a few days. I rose and fell a little, lying down, eyes at water level. . . . Willie Gonzales drifted far outside, arms folded, watching the shifts in shadows and holding a kelp strand as an anchor against the current. A seal's shiny head surfaced quietly behind him, undetected. It watched Willie's back for a minute, then leapt out of the water and came down with a terrific slap: thrashing and kicking, Willie spun around on his board, utterly hysterical, face white, screaming, "What was that!? What the *hell* was that!?"

And I didn't blame him: you can think you're thinking only about the super chicken burrito you intend to have for lunch, brush your leg against a thick boa kelp stalk and absolutely flip with terror, find that death by devouring lurks just a thought below your mind's surface. *Sharkiness:* state of mind spoken as a state of place—"Getting kinda sharky out here, dontcha think?"—a combination of a break's history, water depth, and exposure to open ocean, maybe crowd level, fog density, and even just sheer distance from the highway. I paddled over to a patch of kelp to hide from the deep, and, thinking of the guy who'd been dragged around, sat up to avoid decapitation. A neighbor of mine had been sitting on his board near here just recently, thinking what a drag it would be if a shark appeared. There were so few waves, he'd have had to paddle in. And just then, he'd seen a four-foot dorsal fin ten feet away from him, a huge, swirling wake displacing as it moved slowly past. He told me his eyes couldn't quite process it at first, kept trying to see a seal or a sea lion; but then another surfer had *leaned* around the fin and nodded frantically with an expression that said, *Uh huh, that's exactly what you think it is!* As they paddled for the beach, my neighbor turned around once to see the fin slowly following; decided right then not to look back again. When they'd screamed the other surfers ashore, one diehard remained in the water, unbelieving. I had actually mistaken a sea-lion flipper for a fin once and discovered a peculiar human dynamic: guys want to scorn your misplaced fear, are ever ready to laugh at he who cries wolf, but never quite do. The danger is simply too legitimate for teasing. Nearly everyone, no matter how gruff and grim, is scared witless at the thought of being torn apart while conscious, of watching a spreading slick of one's own blood. Nevertheless, Skinny once felt convinced he'd seen a great white inside a wave: he'd paddled for shore and left without telling any of the other ten surfers in the water, didn't want to be ridiculed. But great whites were, after all, nowhere more common than right here on this coast. The patch of ocean from Monterey, just south of where I floated, out to the Farallon Islands off San Francisco and north to Bodega Bay just north of the Golden Gate had become known—in wonderfully oblique terms—as the Red Triangle. And, indeed, I'd been out alone at the Point one morning at just the hour when several surfers sighted a great white less than a mile north.

So many disturbing traits, once you look into them—with a somewhat morbid curiosity, I'd begun prowling around the

University Science Library, an airy new building with gestures toward native construction materials, a self-conscious sensitivity to the surrounding redwoods, and the rational and antiseptic calm of too many quantitative minds padding silently down well-carpeted corridors. A few tidbits: sharks are the world's only known *intrauterine cannibals;* as eggs hatch within a uterus, the unborn young fight and devour each other until one well-adapted predator emerges. (If the womb is a battleground, what then the sea?) Also, without the gas-filled bladders that float other fish, sharks, if they stop swimming, sink. This explains their tendency to lurk along the bottom like twenty-one-foot, 4,600-pound benthic land mines with hundred-year life spans. Hard skin bristling with tiny teeth sheathes their flexible cartilage skeletons—no bone at all. Conical snouts, black eyes without visible pupils, black-tipped pectoral fins. Tearing out and constantly being replaced, their serrated fangs have as many as twenty-eight stacked spares (a bite meter embedded in a slab of meat once measured a dusky shark's bite at eighteen tons per square inch). And all of the following have been found in shark bellies: a goat, a tomcat, three birds, a raincoat, overcoats, a car license plate, grass, tin cans, a cow's head, shoes, leggings, buttons, belts, hens, roosters, a nearly whole reindeer, even a headless human in a full suit of armor. Swimming with their mouths open, great whites are indiscriminate recyclers of the organic—my sensitive disposition, loving family and affection for life, my decent pickup, room full of books, preoccupation with chocolate in the afternoons, and tendency to take things too personally: all immaterial to my status as protein.

Leftovers from premammalian times, survivors of the dinosaur extinction, sharks evolved completely and always in the sea, never in fresh water. First appearing 350 million years ago, they've descended from sixty-foot, fifty-ton prehistoric monsters, truly overdetermined predators—in one photo a group of scientists stands comfortably inside a pair of fossilized jaws. Great whites are capable of between forty and seventy knots—calculated from photographic blur—and one writer describes a diver in the Mediterranean being hit so hard he exploded. Another mentions a white shark leaping clear out of the water to pull a seal off a rock, and writes that "in most attacks, witnesses see neither seal nor shark, only a sudden explosion

blasting spray fifteen feet high, then a slick of blood on the surface." One never sees the white before it strikes, no speeding fin: it surges up in ambush, jaw distended, and tears out fifty-pound chunks of flesh. Death coming truly like a stroke of lightning; in that vast, three-dimensional world of the sea, the surfer's world is quite two-dimensional, all surface and shore, with neither depth nor open sea. Aiding the shark's stealth are jelly-filled subcutaneous canals on its head and sides that are lined with neuromasts called ampullae of Lorenzini, a kind of prey radar detecting faint electrical fields. (As a surfer waits for a wave, his very life force pulses like a homing beacon.) And their powerful eyes—with optic nerves thick as ropes—see detail quite poorly, are adapted only to separating prey from background. Among the world's most efficient predators, great whites have a kill rate better than ninety percent, while the hawks just inland strike all day without luck.

I popped a kelp bulb just as a seal rose and looked at me, processing my presence. Perhaps wondering why I'd be stupid enough to dress like him in this part of town.

"Don't like seeing seals," said a surfer nearby.

Now I was nervous, having always seen seals as good news.

"Just paranoid," he answered, when I asked why, "because . . . I'm Erik Larsen." He sounded almost apologetic.

I looked closely, saw the resemblance to the bandaged figure in the photographs. He rolled up his wetsuit sleeve to show deep scars the length of his forearm; I let a little wave pass—had to ask.

"Kind of foggy out there," he said, telling a much-told tale, "and my brother had just gone in. I got this weird feeling a big animal was under me. Really hoping it was a sea lion. Then I saw teeth, like coming up at me."

Willie drifted over to listen.

"And then my whole leg was in the thing's mouth," Larsen said, slouching like a beaten veteran. "It cut my thigh muscle in half and severed my femoral artery." He looked outside at a three-wave set; clouds still a gray continuum. Willie said he'd heard you bled to death if your femoral artery got cut.

"If you slit it, you do," Larsen said, "but it's like a rubber band, so if you cut it all the way like mine, it'll snap back and close a little."

Not a distinction I enjoyed picturing. Willie looked toward the beach.

Larsen explained how the shark let go, circled, and attacked again, this time at his head. "I put up my arms," he said, crossing them before his face, "and it cut all the adductor tendons and my right brachial artery—the really big one under your bicep. My arms were all flopping around in its mouth. Yeah, I totally remember thinking how much room there was in there, like plenty for me. But I got one arm out and hit it in the eye."

He took a breath. I was stunned, couldn't be patient—and then?

"It let go," he said. "And I actually got on my board. . . . And the miracle is, I could even paddle because I still had the tendons that pulled down, even though it cut the ones that lift up. I actually caught a wave." He laughed a little. "Yeah, a little one. Belly-rode it in, and a lady came out with her kid and I told them how to tie tourniquets. When the chopper got there I'd lost a third of my blood."

The end of the story left an awkward silence: what to say? Larsen stroked into a waist-high right and surfed it casually, did what the wave wanted. I floated awhile alone, then caught one in—waves kind of small, not real interesting.

Daniel Duane *was born in 1967. He is the author of* Lighting Out: A Vision of California and the Mountains, Caught Inside: A Surfer's Year on the California Coast, *and* Looking for Mo. *His work has appeared in the* New York Times, Esquire, Outside, *and the* San Francisco Examiner. *He lives in San Francisco.*

Pacific Coast Storm

MANUEL FIGUROA

Spatters of winter rain
Beat a toy-drum tattoo
On my southern window
Through which I barely see
An outline of the bay.

I am surrounded by
The sounds of this winter
Storm . . . yet . . . what is that call
I hear? *Chir-rup! Chir-rup!*
Frogs in a holly tree—

Almost drowned by
The raging wind,
Tiny voices
Calling, calling.

Log trucks rumble across
The bridge at our corner,
Echoes of thrumming frogs.

Then all, all is silent
But for the sloughing wind.

Manuel Figuroa *grew up in Denver and graduated from Manual Training High School. After serving in the U.S. Air Force, he received his B.A. from Oregon's Reed College. He worked in California for a number of years before moving to Colorado's San Luis Valley, just west of the Sangre de Cristo Mountains.*

The Secret of
C. D. Parkhurst

Felicia Silcox

California history is replete with tales of individuals who were as rugged as the western lands in which they lived. This true story tells of one of the region's especially hardy characters.

During California's booming Gold Rush, people trusted stagecoaches to carry their mail and their strongboxes loaded with fabulous wealth. Passengers rocked from side to side as the cramped vehicles, cradled in leather straps that served as springs, hurtled along narrow dirt roads through rugged terrain.

High in the driver's box, the tough "whips" knew that safe, on-time delivery depended on them. Wrapped in buffalo skin overcoats, their broad-brimmed hats pulled low, drivers peered through dense fog, wind-driven rain, and snow. With loud, throaty whistles, they warned of their approach as they sped toward blind mountain curves.

It was said that a good whip could drive "six mustangs down a grade like the roof of a house, with the hub of one wheel grazing the hillside rock and the tire of the other hanging half over a precipice."

Passengers always arrived safely when "One-Eyed Charley" Parkhurst drove. Strong and compactly built, Charley earned respect for his skill in handling horses and his coolheaded exploits. He had a tan, clean-shaven face and wore a patch over one eye. Fond of children, he was shy around ladies, although he reportedly helped one poor widow buy a ranch.

One rainy winter, according to an 1880 edition of the *San Francisco Chronicle*, Charley's team struggled through mud that reached nearly to the hubs of the stage's wheels. Before him stretched a swollen river spanned by a wooden bridge, its foundation creaking and rocking in the torrent. Barely hesitating, Charley lashed his horses forward. Just as he reached the opposite shore, the bridge "swayed over the stream for a minute and then tumbled into the water."

A shotgun-toting bandit named Sugarfoot once ambushed and robbed Charley. But when the robber and his men tried a second time, the fearless coachman was ready. Shooting left and right, Charley whipped his horses past the gang, leaving Sugarfoot fatally wounded on the road.

Another day, after Charley's team bolted, he was knocked from the driver's box. Clinging to the reins while being dragged along the trail, Charley managed to steer the runaway mustangs into thick roadside chaparral. The coach finally stopped, much to the relief of its terrified occupants.

After years of exposure to cold, damp weather, Charley became crippled with rheumatism. By that time, the railroad— faster and safer than the stagecoach—was beginning to dominate transportation. Charley retired and, for a time, operated a stage rest stop. Later he raised cattle and sometimes worked as a lumberjack. Records show that Charley voted in the 1868 presidential election, won by the former Civil War general, Ulysses S. Grant.

Sometime during the 1870s, Charley sold his cattle ranch

and moved to a small cabin on the ranch of his friends, the Harmon family. The Harmons looked after him until he died in December of 1879 at the age of sixty-seven. In his will, signed "C. D. Parkhurst," Charley left his life savings to the Harmons' young son, George.

But when townsfolk prepared Charley's body for burial, they discovered that their fearless hero was a woman! In an age when ladies wore long skirts, observed "proper" behavior, and fainted from too much excitement, Charley had lived the rugged life of a Wells Fargo whip. Moreover, "C. D. Parkhurst" had voted—fifty-two years before American women won that right in 1920.

A former teacher, editor, and medical assistant, **Felicia Silcox** *finds inspiration for her children's writing by volunteering with local teens and helping her husband raise Navajo-Churros on their sheep ranch in central California.*

For an Encore

KATIE McALLASTER WEAVER

Leaping from
the tips of
pine trees,
squirrels tap
dance on our aluminum
roof, not-so-soft
shoeing down the
sliding slope of
our house and
if it's not
too early in the morning,
usually,
I hope they
live through it
to return again
for an encore
performance.

Katie McAllaster Weaver *is an award-winning poet whose work has appeared in magazines such as* Highlights, Cricket, Ladybug, *and* Cicada, *and in several anthologies. She lives in Benicia, California, with her husband and daughter.*

Earthquake and Fire

KATHRYN HULME

Kathryn Hulme was six years old on April 18, 1906, when a devastating earthquake rocked San Francisco and broke open more than 270 miles of land along the San Andreas Fault. The earthquake, which measured about 7.8 on the Richter scale, was felt as far north as Oregon and as far south as Los Angeles. Several decades later, Hulme turned her memories of the great quake into a chapter for her novel, We Lived as Children, *from which this excerpt is drawn.*

Chandeliers shattered through the house as we snatched at clothes laid out in order for the picnic. We were all in the same room without knowing how we got there. The shocks threw us against the wall, back on the bed. Buzz whimpered, his sweater on backwards. Never mind, never mind. Jen had tears rolling down her cheeks, no sound of crying. My teeth chattered, I clenched my jaw, nothing could stop anything. A far grumble of earth roared to nearness, under the house, under our feet. Timber creaked and crockery pitched off pantry shelves. A crack opened in the wall and spread under our gaze like a vein down to the slats beneath the plaster.

Hurry, hurry, said mother.

We fled down the hall past lurching pictures, stopped in terror as the Alaskan harpoons fell from the antler prongs. We clung together at the head of the stairs watching them wave and twist while the doorframe made a ripping noise. Then mother led the way. She snatched up the picnic hamper as we ran through the door.

We stood dazed in the middle of the street. Neighbors in nightgowns yelled: *No, there!* WHERE?—*The vacant lot—live wires.* We got across just as a telephone pole tumbled, pulling with it a loop of deadly wire. Mother moaned: Oh, oh! as it writhed where our feet had been. We clutched mother speechlessly while the second and third shocks came, feeling her knees shaking under her skirt. The ground rocked. Our own sobs were lost in the shrieks of those still running toward the open space. An underground roar came with each temblor; it didn't seem safe to stand on earth, but there was no place to go.

A sharp twist nearly flung us to the ground, then the rocking stopped. We stared at each other unable to recognize the faces we saw. We stared at the rising sun; even that looked gray and drained with fright like the faces around us. We stood with legs apart waiting for another shock, ears strained for the rumbling. Only sounds of loosened bricks rattling down roofs, crashes of glass, and a queer indrawn sobbing all around us. A little shake came, almost more awful than the twisters because no sound came with it, a quiet tremor like nerves after a convulsion. Then someone said in an everyday voice: It's all over.

We saw Dr. Sonntag embracing his Lena, crying: Gott verdanke, Gott verdanke! He wore only gray wool underdrawers and a striped shirt, but it didn't seem funny. Mr. Percy in pajamas and straw hat came up to mother and said: In another second I was going to come and get you, and we had a sense of a man looking out for us. Mother asked in the smallest voice I ever heard from her: Do you think it's all over? I should say it is, said Mr. Percy; why, that first quake lasted nearly two minutes. He stamped the ground with his carpet slippers and said scornfully: That's all this old earth is capable of in one day. We felt much better. A man would know. Presently his eye fell on the picnic hamper, he stood back in amazement. Say, he said, you folks look as though you'd planned on this. He acted aggrieved. You might have let a neighbor in on the secret, he said. Then he went around telling everyone that we knew the earthquake was coming, we even packed a picnic lunch for it. He brought the first smiles and walked off like a hero, saying: I'm going to get my clothes.

We'll sit down and wait awhile, mother said; Buzz, you spread out the coats. No, I know, we'll all help, she said, pretending not to notice his shaking hands. Jen was white, but her hands were steady. We sat close together, the thumping of the heart and the trembling seemed less with our bodies touching. I was the only one with a peculiarity unshared. My teeth chattered so I felt I ought to apologize.

I ca-a-n't m-m-m-ake them st-st-stop, I tried to say.

Buzz, hearing such sounds, lifted his head from mother's lap and looked with interest at my chattering teeth. Gee whizz, ma, he said, she'll knock out all her teeth.

After a while it was fun looking around seeing what people had snatched up in their dash from houses. One woman held a Bohemian glass bowl—But no food in it, Jen remarked like an observant housekeeper. When we looked over the bird-cages, both parrot and canary, the clocks, bed pillows, and coal-scuttles our neighbors had picked up, nothing anyone could eat, we felt quite superior about mother's choice of picnic hamper. Also, we were properly dressed. We began making fun

of the half-clads. Mother had to hush us, but she did it with encouraging pats as if to say: I'll be with you in a minute just as soon as I'm sure . . . while her eyes searched the overcast sky like an anxious mariner's.

The vacant lot where we sat was the end of civilization. Behind us rolled grassy fields lifting finally to Twin Peaks. The Statue of Liberty hill was nearer, beginning almost in our backyard. Only the hills looked as if nothing had happened. Our street was scattered with shingles and stair railings, chimneys and window-panes, and one house three doors down from us had had an entire side wall shaken off so that it was like looking into a large-scale dollhouse, kitchen, dining-room, and parlor downstairs, bedrooms above with a brass bedstead hanging over the open edge—Clinging by its castors, mother said, and for some reason made my brother remember our cat.

Alfred! He raised up. One of us was missing. I'm going to get Alfred, he said.

Mother said: I'll go, and started to rise.

Buzz had been listening to the men ordering their women-folk about. He fixed mother with a look. You stay here, ma—there were tears in his eyes he was so frightened to go back to the house alone—I can get Alfred quicker, he said, he answers my whistle.

Mother held him. Is it all right, do you think? she asked Mr. Short, the wholesale grocer whose family camped next to us.

Sure, it's all over, said Mr. Short, let the kid go, it'll do him good. But say, sonny, he said to Buzz, steer wide around those wires, they haven't cut the current yet.

Don't go in the house, dear, just stand in the backyard and whistle, mother said. Buzz kissed her the way he'd seen the men do and walked toward the house, his half-laced leggings flapping.

Mother's eyes went out after him like guiding hands. We saw him go into the narrow alley that led to the backyard. He didn't look much taller than the calla lilies.

Fine son you've got there, Mr. Short said to mother; that's what I like to see. He had three daughters. Mother answered him without taking her eyes from the empty alleyway. We heard a thin whistle. I thought jealously: I wouldn't have been able to whistle with these chattering teeth . . . then we felt it, a tremor that started the noises again in all the houses. Before we got to our feet the shock reached its peak, splitting and crashing. Mr. Short held mother. The brass bed fell off the floor edge of the unfinished house.

You can't, you can't, he yelled. Just as mother broke away, Buzz came round the corner of the house, vomiting violently every few steps, the cat dragging from his clenched arm. The earthquake was over by the time he reached us.

Jen took the cat, and mother took Buzz. None of us said anything on account of his face. It had been the end of the world to him there alone in the yard. When he could speak he told us the back stairs had come off the house. They fell off, ma, he stuttered. The kitchen door looked so funny all alone. Alfred was scared to death. The red claw-marks showed he still had blood in his body.

I'd have been terribly scared, I chattered.

Oh, you, a girl, Buzz said, and mother held him over while he retched again.

The militia moved into the cow hollows beyond the end of our street. We watched their white tents go up in rows. The flag they hoisted disappointed us a little; it wouldn't float on the breeze, because there was no breeze. The heavy atmosphere hung with a dangerous stillness as if waiting. We didn't realize for a long time that the murk we saw in one corner of the sky was smoke.

A horse cab appeared at the foot of our street. We watched it wind up the hill round the wreckage bringing Mr. Percy's sister back to the parent home. As the cabby deposited his fare and turned his horse, he shouted to us: The whole town's a-burnin'. He waved his whip and drove down the hill to get more refugees.

Fire! We had been so absorbed in our own block-length world we had almost forgotten the rest of the city. Refugees, ruins, burst gas mains, fire, fire, fire. The words flashed through our group from man to man. We heard mother repeat each one in a whisper. Bucket brigades, martial law, ten thousand refugees, twenty thousand, it went beyond our scope. Jen knew about some of it, but Buzz and I couldn't get beyond the word *fire*. We shivered with excitement. The biggest fire we'd ever seen was when a row of three flats burned down. The whole city, Buzz murmured, his feverish eyes lifting to the hill, picking his seat for the sight.

His fever increased so that we couldn't go up the hill that night with the neighbors. We went back to the house early and mother put him to bed. . . .

Next morning wasn't like a beginning of day, there was a tired light. Sheets still hanging from our clothesline in the backyard were covered with bits of charred paper. Jen and I ran outside to look, we had slept in our clothes and did not have to dress.

Ashes and charred bits were falling from the sky, coming so slowly they looked motionless in the air. The particles didn't seem of earth, you could imagine something high up in the sky had been on fire the night before.

It's a big fire, Jen said, and wet her finger to see if there was any wind.

Neighbors were climbing the hill behind our house. They went up single file carrying small bundles. Around the base of the statue was a crowd of people who had come up from the Mission district. We ran back to the house with the news.

Buzz was gnawing cold chicken, looking as if he had never had a sick day in his life. He was dressed in extra sweaters and mother had put a cape over his shoulders and pulled the pointed hood over his head. She was rolling up bedding by the front door. Jen and I carried down food from the pantry. All together it made such a load that mother said we'd have to have a horse if we had to leave in a hurry. She was trying to be casual so Buzz wouldn't run up another fever of fright. She really didn't need to worry. The prospect of no more houses excited us.

I know just where we can camp, Buzz said, that old quarry halfway up Twin Peaks. I argued for a place nearer Sutro Forest so we could find mushrooms when our store food was eaten. We almost came to blows while mother was tying a twenty-dollar gold piece in a handkerchief and pinning it to her corset. Don't squabble, we're not burned out *yet*, she said.

Not yet . . . we started toward the hill with the last of the stragglers, hearing those words on all sides. Buzz and I scrambled ahead as if the fire might go out and there would be nothing to see from the hill. We had promised mother we would wait for her near the top. She came up with Jen faster than any of the others, she didn't have to put her hands down and come on all fours over the steep places. She'll be good, camping, Buzz said.

The fire was so big we couldn't think of it as a fire at first. There was no beginning or end, it spread over the downtown district from the Mission to the Golden Gate in such a wide arc we had to turn our heads to see it all. It was too big even for Buzz; he sat like the rest of us, staring. . . .

A man, a stranger from the other side of the hill, said: They'll dynamite, try to stop it jumping Van Ness Avenue.

Dynamite. Buzz and I looked at each other in an explosion of glances. . . .

I thought the dynamiting would relieve the sadness, but it didn't. Buildings went up in air, dropping apart in fragments that showered down like fireworks. Each time it happened there was a comment.

There goes the Phelan Building.

That's the Crocker Bank, oh, my God.

A superb skyrocket flew high from a bed of fire and turned into a parachute of embers.

Spreckels, the dead voice said, and scraps of ash fell off the shaking heads of those who couldn't speak.

Mother's tears dropped in her lap. She couldn't look at the exploding buildings the way we children did. Men around us were crying like mother, not because they had a business down there or money in the melting bank vaults, they didn't mention those; but because it was their background being blown up.

It's going to jump the firebreak anyhow, a voice said.

A wind began to blow in from the Bay. Smoke pointed the direction of it, inland toward our hills. People from the Mission district started down their side of the hill to fetch the belongings which, like us, they had left piled by front doors.

It's blowing away from the waterfront, Jen said, bringing father again to our thoughts. Perhaps over there on the other side of the smoke he was watching the new direction of the fire, thinking of us. I knew instinctively that we would see him that night, though when I looked at the flames that separated us I didn't see how he would get through.

By afternoon the fire had spread to the Mission. There were still dozens of blocks of houses between the foot of our hill and the flames, but we could smell the smoke now.

If it gets as far as Mission Dolores, Mr. Percy said, then we're goners. Mother motioned him to sit down beside her. They started talking together.

Only one place, one place, we heard mother say.

Not Golden Gate Park, thousands there, danger of pestilence, Mr. Percy said.

No, no, the hills, mother whispered. It was a plot. We saw them move closer so none of the others could overhear. Mr. Percy listened to mother with admiration. We felt proud of her; she had a plan no man had thought of. He asked her a question and we heard her say: The children will know that. She beckoned to us.

When were you children last at the reservoir? she whispered.

Jen said: Not for months—but Buzz and I began to tremble. It was such an unexpected question. Only a week ago we had been playing round that forbidden place in the hollow below Twin Peaks. We had climbed over the barbed wire surrounding the open reservoir and had had a terrible experience. I caught a stern look from Mr. Percy, no use to tell a lie.

Last week, I answered.

Was there much water in it? mother asked. Buzz looked off toward the fire.

A little, I said, not very much.

But *how* much? mother insisted.

I could think only of one way to describe the depth. I said: Well, it's not over a child's head. Buzz paled.

Are you sure? How do you know? Mr. Percy asked.

Buzz felt there was no hope left; the tassel on the top of his hood shook as he said: Because I fell in.

Mother's laugh bewildered us. I thought they'd know, she said to Mr. Percy, and he laughed too. We were sent off without a scolding. The low-toned conversation continued, we couldn't catch any more words. The Short family was sitting near by, augmented by relatives from downtown. We could see that mother was being careful that they should not overhear her plan.

As the fire moved closer other families on the hill were making plans too, drawing apart, whispering, and writing down lists of provisions. Buzz and I walked around pretending to be searching better viewpoints for the fire. Within an hour we knew where every family in the neighborhood was planning to run if the fire broke over the hill, except our own.

Mother watched now with measuring eyes, getting opinions from the men as to whether it would reach the base of the hill during the night. Mr. Percy and his sister stood with her, a close three guarding a secret from the rabble that had been streaming up the hill all morning. I could see there were quite a few people one wouldn't want to live with in a cave for several days.

That night mother told us. We had gone back to the wrecked house where the baskets of food were hidden. We were sitting on the front porch with slices of my brother's birthday cake in our hands, dropping crumbs and not caring. Mother looked reckless and wild with her hair blown and no plate under her cake. Jen ate delicately as if she were at a party, she didn't have a spot on her dress from our day's living on the hilltop.

Mother said: I'm going to tell you children a secret; it's something we'll do, just in case . . . she lifted her face to the sky where the arc of red cut across. You mustn't tell a soul, she said, there wouldn't be room, only for us and the Percys. We crossed our hearts and leaned toward her. She paused a moment, looked at the three of us one by one, said: Oh, like a quick embrace, then continued: *If* the fire should break over the hill tonight, we're going up to the reservoir. Buzz and I looked guiltily at each other. Mother shook her finger at him and said: I remember that day you came home rough dried. Well, she went on, we might go up to the reservoir and *fall in again.*

We were too excited to speak. The magnificence of her plan stunned us. We saw ourselves standing chin-deep in water while flames raged overhead. Then Jen spoke: But, mother, you get sick just as soon as water touches your stomach. That was true; we suddenly recalled mother's terror of water, all the vacation-time creeks she had bathed in and how, when we pulled her into waist-deep places, she grew pale with fright and was sick. It was one of our family jokes—You, the daughter of a sea captain, we used to say.

Mother seemed glad that Jen had thought of that; she patted her and said: No, I'd promise not to get sick, I could stand it for a little while, I really wouldn't be a coward, especially if you children were not afraid.

Oh no, we cried. Afraid? How could she ever imagine we would be afraid?

You can't wade in, you know, Buzz said expertly. When you once get in it's all the same, up to here. He touched his throat and made me remember how he looked that day when another six inches would have drowned him. And also, he said, you've got the barbed wire to think of.

Barbed wire? Mother looked defeated.

Yes, all around the reservoir, Buzz said. He looked at her, wondering how far he could go, then threw all caution to the winds. But a good thick pad of newspaper will fix that, he said, that's the way we always get over barbed wire.

It was quite wonderful to be able to give away our secrets to mother, to have her so unexpectedly grateful for all the knowledge we had acquired on our trespassing expeditions. We told her everything we knew about the reservoir, the best trails up to it, how rain collected in it, deepening it inch by inch all winter, and spring freshets feeding it from the hills. It was an abandoned reservoir; after it was built it was found to be not high enough to supply the necessary pressure. It has no outlet, Buzz said.

Mother picked a piece of icing off her cake, pretending to examine its consistency. Has it got *things* in it? she asked.

Not a sign of life, we assured her. We could speak with the authority of fishermen. Only lily pads floating around, we said, and mother shivered and looked at the sky.

When Mr. Percy passed on the way back to his house we waved to him and sang out: *Mother, may I go out to swim?* to let him know we knew the secret, and he sang back: *Yes, my darling daughter,* quick and responsive in the way we liked. That'll be our password, Buzz said.

How does it look? mother called down to him.

They're backfiring, maybe it'll hold, Mr. Percy said, but if not . . . he gave us a significant wave. He would come for us. We had everything ready, four packages of food graded in size, the largest for mother, the next for Jen and smaller ones for my brother and me. I didn't see how we were going to be able to sleep that night. We studied the sky before we went indoors.

It looks a little redder, Buzz said hopefully.

Mother tucked us in bed fully dressed and said she was going out to sit on the porch for a while. Jen and I lay together listening to Buzz's breathing and the murmur of voices from the porch.

Isn't it exciting? I whispered. Will we undress for it, do you suppose? and I floated from her arms into the reservoir and made everybody laugh when I rested my elbows on two lily pads as if they were little green tables.

Laura, are you all right? It was my father's voice on our front porch, strained and anxious. . . .

Next morning militiamen brought the bodies down from the reservoir. We watched them winding single file down the trail, wondering what they carried wrapped in two khaki army blankets. Everyone guessed aloud until the soldiers were in our street, then we knew, and no one could speak. Two refugee children from the burning Mission, separated from their family in the flight from the flames, had gone up alone to the reservoir the night before. The soldiers spoke tersely as they tramped along. A water main in the hill had burst, filling the reservoir. They had been sent up to investigate. At first they thought the floating faces were water lilies. Mother stood rigid as the damp bundles went by, then suddenly she crumpled as if every bone in her body had dissolved, falling softly at our feet.

Born in San Francisco in 1900, **Kathryn Hulme** *had a varied career that included working as an electric welder during World War II and later serving as deputy director of the United Nations Relief and Refugee Association field teams. She wrote many articles and several books of fiction and nonfiction.*

Mysteries

T. H. WATKINS

As a boy, T. H. Watkins traveled each summer with his mother, father, two brothers, and two sisters to the beaches near San Juan Capistrano for a three-week camping vacation. The following excerpt describes one of his early morning rituals when he was about ten or eleven years old.

Morning: You had no way of knowing precisely what it was that woke you, whether it was the moist touch of wind laced with fog, the sound of the surf or just the peevish squawk of gulls as they flocked for breakfast. Whatever it was, you woke suddenly, like a businessman in a hotel room in a strange city. For a while you lay in the folded warmth of your sleeping bag and contemplated the day, while your dog, who had squirmed in with you at some point during the night, grunted comfortably as you squeezed her closer to you. If the day was typical, it would be about six o'clock in the morning. The top of your bag would be beaded with moisture, and overhead you would see the dank, gray clouds of overcast marching off toward the horizon like a series of lumpy, upside-down hills. Beneath the clouds, the slate-blue sea moved like oil, shrugging itself into halfhearted waves that dribbled quickly into foam, collapsing more with a sigh than a crash.

If the tide was out, as it often was, you did not lie in the bag for too long, for there would be things to see. Flushing the dog out, you wriggled into your blue jeans and sweat shirt, which had been tucked into the foot of the bag the night before to keep them warm and dry. You then tiptoed ever so quietly into the camp and grabbed your sand bucket. In their trailer-bedroom your mother and father made a single great lump from which emanated a duet of murmurous snoring. From the tent where the rest of the family lay, there came no sound at all. They would all be good for another two or three hours, and you sneaked back out of camp and ran—raced—toward the exposed rocks and tide pools at the foot of the small point that lay perhaps a mile away.

You ran, dog at your side, not just to keep warm or for the simple joy of it, but because you wanted to take advantage of every secret moment of this time. Your parents had not forbidden these unsupervised expeditions; they simply did not know about them, and you wanted to keep it that way. God knew, it was dangerous enough a business, clambering barefoot over rocks polished by centuries of beating surf, made slick, smooth, and wet. One slip, and you could break an arm or leg, or even crack your skull. And if you were injured as far out on those rocks as you frequently ventured, you could lie immobilized until the tide returned and the sea washed your body away—and no one to know where you were. If you thought about it, it could all be pretty frightening—but of course you did not think about it. Your step was sure and unhesitant, your confidence boundless, your good luck remarkable.

And it was worth it, for this rocky landscape, stripped of the sea which kept it hidden for most of the day, vibrated with a secret, mysterious, unimaginable life that creeped and crawled in its pools, its dark nooks and crannies, like a population straight out of dream. Where else but out of the mists of dream could a hermit crab have been spawned? Barely an inch in length, he scrabbled and lurched among the rocks, seeking an unoccupied shell to inhabit; without it, he was a pitiful, help-less creature, his pink lower body curled under his torso like a tiny coil of rope; with it, he lurched along as before—quite as helpless, but at least granted the illusion of security. Starfish, too, were dream-like, inching through life on those impossible arms, changing colors to match their surroundings, their mouths a tiny slit in the bottom center of their bodies, where mouths had no business being. And more: crabs, pink ones the size of dinner plates with pincers that could hurt, if not maim; mottled yellow ones as broad as the palm of your hand, little sand-colored ones no larger than your thumbnail; mussels and sea-snails clustered on the sides of rocks, extensions of the stone itself, immobile, hiding from the light, waiting for the re-turn of the tide and their real world; an occasional landlocked ray trying to hide itself behind a rock in a tide pool and once in a while a smelt or a rock fish, or a gang of herring that had become similarly trapped; nearly invisible sea worms that squiggled along the bottom of pools like miniature snakes; and, most wondrous of all, the rainbow-colored anemones, half-animal, half-flower, lurking in rock crannies with poison at the heart of their beauty. Over it all the ubiquitous gulls wheeled and screamed, small shadows of death that harvested what they could of that abundance of life.

You were entranced, utterly. Leaping from rock to rock, tide pool to tide pool, you poked and probed and watched everything you could watch. Lying on your belly at the edge of a particularly rich pool, you would be driven by the small boy's insatiable need to know, to understand, to experience—in

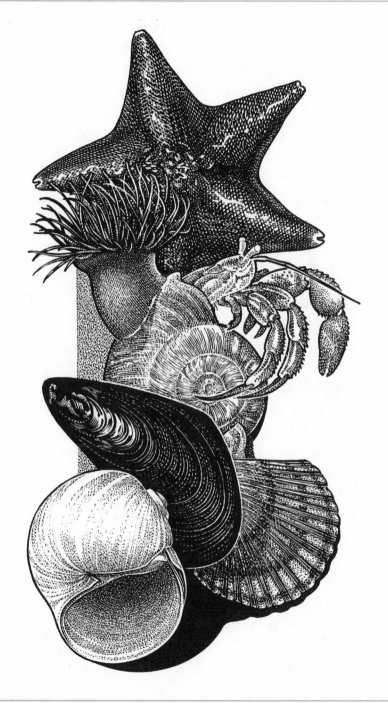

short, to meddle. You would take out your little tin shovel from the sand bucket and use it to stir up a sleeping ray, if you could reach him. You would use it to stroke the petals of a crimson anemone, shuddering as the petals convulsed in an attempt to draw the shovel into its maw; thus you discovered that beauty could be a trap—a very large thing to learn at so young an age. You would seek out a large crab and toy with it until in its rage and fear it gripped the shovel firmly. You would then lift it out of the pool and dump it in your bucket, captured, helpless to escape the mindless cruelty of your curiosity. For you it was a game, for him a death struggle.

No matter how often or how long you visited this secret world, the potential for surprise was never absent—and it could sometimes be a large surprise, indeed. Once you discovered the body of a sea lion stranded on the edge of a tide pool far out among the rocks. You came upon it suddenly, unexpectedly, while crawling over the lip of a rock, and at first you thought it was alive. But no: the gulls had already been at its eyes. It was a huge mound of blue-black flesh, perhaps six or seven feet from nose to tail. You poked at the still resilient flesh with your shovel—gingerly, and a little fearfully. This was not your first dramatic encounter with death; after all, you had watched gulls hammering and picking at still-living crabs, a grisly and unforgettable spectacle. But never before had you realized the sheer power of a force that could destroy even this human-sized creature, leaving it to be picked at by gulls and crabs and whatever other scavengers there were who did the sea's bone-cleaning. To stand too close to it was to stand too close to your own end. You left it finally, left it for the sea that would reclaim it in a few hours.

Perhaps it was nothing more complicated than your stomach-clock sounding an alarm for food, but you always seemed to know when it was time to head back to camp. You dumped whatever creatures you might have in your bucket back into their tide pool and scrambled back across the rocks to the beach where your dog would be waiting (she possessed no measurable interest in tide pools or slippery rocks). Running along the beach (when did you not run?) you stopped now and then to scoop up a few shells, for you had to have some reasonable excuse for your long absence. *Where in the world have you been? Shells,* you could say, holding out your bucket. *I've been collecting shells.* The answer would suffice, for there was neither danger nor mystery in shell-collecting.

⌣

T. H. Watkins *worked for many years as the editor of* Wilderness, *the magazine of the Wilderness Society. He wrote eighteen books on history or the environment, including* California: An Illustrated History.

Great Places

Hollywood and the Pits

CHERYLENE LEE

Between forty thousand and eight thousand years ago, mammoths, mastodons, and a host of other animals became trapped in a pit of tar located in what is now downtown Los Angeles. Today the La Brea Tar Pits, protected as a park, stand in sharp contrast to the glamorous show business world around them. Or do they?

In 1968 when I was fifteen, the pit opened its secret to me. I breathed, ate, slept, dreamed about the La Brea Tar Pits. I spent summer days working the archaeological dig and, in dreams, saw the bones glistening, the broken pelvises, the skulls, the vertebrae looped like a woman's pearls hanging on an invisible cord. I welcomed those dreams. I wanted to know where the next skeleton was, identify it, record its position, discover whether it was whole or not. I wanted to know where to dig in the coarse, black, gooey sand. I lost myself there and found something else.

My mother thought something was wrong with me. Was it good for a teenager to be fascinated by death? Especially animal death in the Pleistocene? Was it normal to be so obsessed by a sticky brown hole in the ground in the center of Los Angeles? I don't know if it was normal or not, but it seemed perfectly logical to me. After all, I grew up in Hollywood, a place where dreams and nightmares can often take the same shape. What else would a child actor do?

"Thank you very much, dear. We'll be letting you know."

I knew what that meant. It meant I would never hear from them again. I didn't get the job. I heard that phrase a lot that year.

I walked out of the plush office, leaving behind the casting director, writer, and whoever else came to listen to my reading for a semiregular role on a family sitcom. The carpet made no sound when I opened and shut the door.

I passed the other girls waiting in the reception room, each poring over her script. The mothers were waiting in a separate room, chattering about their daughters' latest commercials, interviews, callbacks, jobs. It sounded like every Oriental kid in Hollywood was working except me.

My mother used to have a lot to say in those waiting rooms. Ever since I was three, when I started at the Meglin Kiddie Dance Studio, I was dubbed "the Chinese Shirley Temple"—always the one to be picked at auditions and interviews, always the one to get the speaking lines, always called "the one-shot kid" because I could do my scenes in one take, even tight close-ups. My mother would talk about me only behind my back because she didn't want me to hear her brag, but I knew that she was proud. In a way I was proud too, though I never dared admit it. I didn't want to be called a show-off. But I didn't exactly know what I did to be proud of either. I only knew that at fifteen I was now being passed over at all these interviews when before I would have been chosen.

My mother looked at my face hopefully when I came into

the room. I gave her a quick shake of the head. She looked bewildered. I felt bad for my mother then. How could I explain it to her? I didn't understand it myself. We left saying polite good-byes to all the other mothers.

We didn't say anything until the studio parking lot, where we had to search for our old blue Chevy among rows and rows of parked cars baking in the Hollywood heat.

"How did it go? Did you read clearly? Did you tell them you're available?"

"I don't think they care if I'm available or not, Ma."

"Didn't you read well? Did you remember to look up so they could see your eyes? Did they ask you if you could play the piano? Did you tell them you could learn?"

The barrage of questions stopped when we finally spotted our car. I didn't answer her. My mother asked about the piano because I lost out in an audition once to a Chinese girl who knew how to play.

My mother took off the towel that shielded the steering wheel from the heat. "You're getting to be such a big girl," she said, starting the car in neutral. "But don't worry, there's always next time. You have what it takes. That's special." She put the car into forward and we drove through a parking lot that had an endless number of identical cars all facing the same direction. We drove back home in silence.

In the La Brea Tar Pits many of the excavated bones belong to juvenile mammals. Thousands of years ago thirsty young animals in the area were drawn to watering holes not knowing they were traps. Those inviting pools had false bottoms made of sticky tar, which immobilized its victims and preserved their bones when they died. Innocence trapped by ignorance. The tar pits record that well.

I suppose a lot of my getting into show business in the first place was a matter of luck—being in the right place at the right time. My sister, seven years older than I, was a member of the Meglin Kiddie Dance Studio long before I started lessons. During one of the annual recitals held at the Shrine Auditorium she was spotted by a Hollywood agent who handled only Oriental performers. The agent sent my sister out for a role in the CBS *Playhouse 90* television production "The Family Nobody Wanted." The producer said she was too tall for the part. But true to my mother's training of always having a positive reply, my sister said to the producer, "But I have a younger sister . . . ," which started my showbiz career at the tender age of three.

My sister and I were lucky. We enjoyed singing and dancing, we were natural hams, and our parents never discouraged us. In fact they were our biggest fans. My mother chauffeured us to all our dance lessons, lessons we begged to take. She drove us to interviews, took us to studios, went on location with us, drilled us on our lines, and made sure we kept up our schoolwork and didn't sass back the tutors hired by studios to teach us for three hours a day. She never complained about being a stage mother. She said that we made her proud.

My father must have felt pride too, because he paid for a choreographer to put together our sister act: "The World Famous Lee Sisters," fifteen minutes of song and dance, real vaudeville stuff. We joked about that a lot, "Yeah, the Lee sisters—Ug-Lee and Home-Lee," but we definitely had a good time. So did our parents. Our father especially liked our getting booked into Las Vegas at the New Frontier Hotel on the Strip. He liked to gamble there, though he said the craps tables in that hotel were "cold," not like the casinos in downtown Las Vegas, where all the "hot" action took place.

In Las Vegas our sister act was part of a show called "Oriental Holiday." The show was about a Hollywood producer going to the Far East, finding undiscovered talent, and bringing it back to the U.S. We did two shows a night in the main showroom, one at eight and one at twelve, and on weekends a third show at two in the morning. It ran the entire summer often to standing-room only audiences—a thousand people a show.

Our sister act worked because of the age and height difference. My sister then was fourteen and nearly five foot two; I was seven and very small for my age—people thought we were cute. We had song-and-dance routines to old tunes like "Ma, He's Making Eyes at Me," "Together," and "I'm Following You," and my father hired a writer to adapt the lyrics to "I Enjoy Being a Girl," which came out "We Enjoy Being Chinese." We also told corny jokes, but the Las Vegas audience seemed to enjoy it. Here we were, two kids, staying up late and jumping around, and getting paid besides. To me the applause sometimes sounded like static, sometimes like distant waves. It always amazed me when people applauded. The owner of the hotel liked us so much, he invited us back to perform in shows for three summers in a row. That was before I grew too tall and the sister act didn't seem so cute anymore.

Many of the skeletons in the tar pits are found incomplete—particularly the skeletons of the young, which have only soft cartilage connecting the bones. In life the soft tissue allows for growth, but in death it dissolves quickly. Thus the skeletons of young animals are more apt to be scattered, especially the vertebrae protecting the spinal cord. In the tar pits, the central ends of many vertebrae are found unconnected to any skeleton. Such bone fragments are shaped like valentines, disks that are slightly lobed—heart-shaped shields that have lost their connection to what they were meant to protect.

I never felt my mother pushed me to do something I didn't want to do. But I always knew if something I did pleased her. She was generous with her praise, and I was sensitive when she withheld it. I didn't like to disappoint her.

I took to performing easily, and since I had started out so young, making movies or doing shows didn't feel like anything special. It was a part of my childhood—like going to the dentist one morning or going to school the next. I didn't wonder if I wanted a particular role or wanted to be in a show or how I would feel if I didn't get in. Until I was fifteen, it never occurred to me that one day I wouldn't get parts or that I might not "have what it takes."

When I was younger, I got a lot of roles because I was so small for my age. When I was nine years old, I could pass for five or six. I was really short. I was always teased about it when I was in elementary school, but I didn't mind because my height got me movie jobs. I could read and memorize lines that actual five-year-olds couldn't. My mother told people she made me sleep in a drawer so I wouldn't grow any bigger.

But when I turned fifteen, it was as if my body, which hadn't grown for so many years, suddenly made up for lost time. I grew five inches in seven months. My mother was amazed. Even I couldn't get used to it. I kept knocking into things, my clothes didn't fit right, and I felt awkward and clumsy when I moved. Dumb things that I had gotten away with, like paying children's prices at the movies instead of junior admission, I couldn't do anymore. I wasn't a shrimp or a small fry any longer. I was suddenly normal.

Before that summer my mother had always claimed she wanted me to be normal. She didn't want me to become spoiled by the attention I received when I was working at the studios. I still had chores to do at home, went to public school when I wasn't working, was punished severely when I behaved badly. She didn't want me to feel I was different just because I was in the movies. When I was eight, I was interviewed by a reporter who wanted to know if I thought I had a big head.

"Sure," I said.

"No you don't," my mother interrupted, which was really unusual because she generally never said anything. She wanted me to speak for myself.

I didn't understand the question. My sister had always made fun of my head. She said my body was too tiny for the weight—I looked like a walking Tootsie Pop. I thought the reporter was making the same observation.

"She better not get that way," my mother said fiercely. "She's not any different from anyone else. She's just lucky and small for her age."

The reporter turned to my mother. "Some parents push their children to act. The kids feel like they're used."

"I don't do that—I'm not that way," my mother told the reporter.

But when she was sitting silently in all those waiting rooms while I was being turned down for one job after another, I could almost feel her wanting to shout, "Use her. Use her. What is wrong with her? Doesn't she have it anymore?" I didn't know what I had had that I didn't seem to have anymore. My mother had told the reporter that I was like everyone else. But when my life was like everyone else's, why was she disappointed?

The churning action of the La Brea Tar Pits makes interpreting the record of past events extremely difficult. The usual order of deposition— the oldest on the bottom, the youngest on the top—loses all meaning when some of the oldest fossils can be brought to the surface by the movement of natural gas. One must look for an undisturbed spot, a place untouched by the action of underground springs or natural gas or human interference. Complete skeletons become important because they indicate areas of least disturbance. But such spots of calm are rare. Whole blocks of the tar pit can become displaced, making false sequences of the past, skewing the interpretation for what is the true order of nature.

That year before my sixteenth birthday, my mother seemed to spend a lot of time looking through my old scrapbooks, staring at all the eight-by-ten glossies from the shows that I had done. In the summer we visited with my grandmother often since I wasn't working and had lots of free time. I would go out to the garden to read or sunbathe, but I could hear my mother and grandmother talking.

"She was so cute back then. She worked with Gene Kelly when she was five years old. She was so smart for her age. I don't know what's wrong with her."

"She's fifteen."

"She's too young to be an ingenue and too old to be cute. The studios forget so quickly. By the time she's old enough to play an ingenue, they won't remember her."

"Does she have to work in the movies? Hand me the scissors."

My grandmother was making false eyelashes using the hair from her hairbrush. When she was young she had incredible hair. I saw an old photograph of her when it flowed beyond her waist like a cascading black waterfall. At seventy, her hair was still black as night, which made her few strands of silver look like shooting stars. But her hair had thinned greatly with age. It sometimes fell out in clumps. She wore it brushed back in a bun with a hairpiece for added fullness. My grandmother had always been proud of her hair, but once she started making false eyelashes from it, she wasn't proud of the way it looked anymore. She said she was proud of it now because it made her useful.

It was painstaking work—tying knots into strands of hair, then tying them together to form feathery little crescents. Her glamorous false eyelashes were much sought after. Theatrical makeup artists waited months for her work. But my grandmother said what she liked was that she was doing something, making a contribution, and besides it didn't cost her anything. No overhead. "Till I go bald," she often joked.

She tried to teach me her art that summer, but for some reason strands of my hair wouldn't stay tied in knots.

"Too springy," my grandmother said. "Your hair is still too young." And because I was frustrated then, frustrated with everything about my life, she added, "You have to wait until your hair falls out, like mine. Something to look forward to, eh?" She had laughed and patted my hand.

My mother was going on and on about my lack of work, what might be wrong, that something she couldn't quite put her finger on. I heard my grandmother reply, but I didn't catch it all: "Movies are just make-believe, not real life. Like what I make with my hair that falls out—false. False eyelashes. Not meant to last."

The remains in the La Brea Tar Pits are mostly of carnivorous animals. Very few herbivores are found—the ratio is five to one, a perversion of the natural food chain. The ratio is easy to explain. Thousands of years ago a thirsty animal sought a drink from the pools of water only to find itself trapped by the bottom, gooey with subterranean oil. A shriek of agony from the trapped victim drew flesh-eating predators, which were then trapped themselves by the very same ooze that provided the bait. The cycle repeated itself countless times. The number of victims grew, lured by the image of easy food, the deception of an easy kill. The animals piled on top of one another. For over ten thousand years the promise of the place drew animals of all sorts, mostly predators and scavengers—dire wolves, panthers, coyotes, vultures—all hungry for their chance. Most were sucked down against their will in those watering holes destined to be called the La Brea Tar Pits in a place to be named the City of Angels, home of Hollywood movie stars.

I spent a lot of time by myself that summer, wondering what it was that I didn't have anymore. Could I get it back? How could I if I didn't know what it was?

That's when I discovered the La Brea Tar Pits, hidden behind the County Art Museum on trendy Wilshire Boulevard. I found a job that didn't require me to be small or cute for my age. I didn't have to audition. No one said, "Thank you very much, we'll call you." Or if they did, they meant it. I volunteered my time one afternoon, and my fascination stuck—like tar on the bones of a saber-toothed tiger.

My mother didn't understand what had changed me. I didn't understand it myself. But I liked going to the La Brea Tar Pits. It meant I could get really messy and I was doing it with a purpose. I didn't feel awkward there. I could wear old stained pants. I could wear T-shirts with holes in them. I could wear disgustingly filthy sneakers and it was all perfectly justified. It wasn't a costume for a role in a film or a part in a TV sitcom. My mother didn't mind my dressing like that when she knew I was off to the pits. That was okay so long as I didn't track tar back into the house. I started going to the pits every day, and my mother wondered why. She couldn't believe I would rather be groveling in tar than going to auditions or interviews.

While my mother wasn't proud of the La Brea Tar Pits (she didn't know or care what a fossil was), she didn't discourage me either. She drove me there, the same way she used to drive me to the studios.

"Wouldn't you rather be doing a show in Las Vegas than scrambling around in a pit?" she asked.

"I'm not in a show in Las Vegas, Ma. The Lee Sisters are retired." My older sister had married and was starting a family of her own.

"But if you could choose between . . ."

"There isn't a choice."

"You really like this tar pit stuff, or are you just waiting until you can get real work in the movies?"

I didn't answer.

My mother sighed. "You could do it if you wanted, if you really wanted. You still have what it takes."

I didn't know about that. But then, I couldn't explain what drew me to the tar pits either. Maybe it was the bones, finding out what they were, which animal they belonged to, imagining how they got there, how they fell into the trap. I wondered about that a lot.

At the La Brea Tar Pits, everything dug out of the pit is saved—including the sticky sand that covered the bones through the ages. Each bucket of sand is washed, sieved, and examined for pollen grains, insect remains, any evidence of past life. Even the grain size is recorded—the percentage of silt to sand to gravel that reveals the history of deposition, erosion, and disturbance. No single fossil, no one observation, is significant enough to tell the entire story. All the evidence must be weighed before a semblance of truth emerges.

The tar pits had their lessons. I was learning I had to work slowly, become observant, concentrate. I learned about time in a way that I would never experience—not in hours, days, and months, but in thousands and thousands of years. I imagined what the past must have been like, envisioned Los Angeles as a sweeping basin, perhaps slightly colder and more humid, a time before people and studios arrived. The tar pits recorded a warming trend; the kinds of animals found there reflected the changing climate. The ones unadapted disappeared. No trace of their kind was found in the area. The ones that adapted to warmer weather left a record of bones in the pit. Amid that collection of ancient skeletons, surrounded by evidence of death, I was finding a secret preserved over thousands and thousands of years. There was something cruel about natural selection and the survival of the fittest. Even those successful individuals that "had what it took" for adaptation still wound up in the pits.

I never found out if I had what it took, not the way my mother meant. But I did adapt to the truth. I wasn't a Chinese Shirley Temple any longer, cute and short for my age. I had grown up. Maybe not on a Hollywood movie set, but in the La Brea Tar Pits.

Cherylene Lee is a Chinese American playwright who also writes stories and poetry.

Fog—San Francisco

VIRGINIA BARRETT

> *The fog comes*
> *on little cat feet.*
> —Carl Sandburg

This fog creeps
on mountain lion paws.

It hunts over the headlands
low bellied and sleek,
its snake tail poised beside the bridge,
then leaps—

Virginia Barrett *lives in San Francisco. Her poems have appeared in anthologies and literary journals, including* Heal Your Soul, Heal the World *(Andrews McMeel, 1998) and* Southern Poetry Review. *She teaches* Hands On Poetry *workshops for adults and* Write Away! *creative writing classes for children and teens.*

Camping Out in Redwood Country

MRS. J. B. RIDEOUT

In 1888, Mrs. J. B. Rideout joined a group of teenagers on a camping trip in northern California. The group traveled from the redwood-covered hills to the coastal town of Mendocino before heading south to Santa Cruz. In these excerpts from her memoir, Camping Out in California, *Mrs. Rideout describes the sights, sounds, dangers, and delights of California redwood country.*

The Gigantic Redwoods

In the month of July I received an invitation to go with a party of young folks. They were to take a large wagon and roam "over the mountains and far away," pitching their tents wherever night found them, and cooking their provisions the old-fashioned way over a camp-fire in a *dutch oven* and a long-handled frying pan.

I must confess I felt dubious about starting, but after the comforting assurances that if we were upset down some steep mountain side, or if wild beasts devoured us, or a band of robbers carried us away, they would all willingly bear me company in each and every trouble, I consented to cast in my lot with the rest.

There were seven of us, but as I have not asked permission,

I shall not give their true names, but will call some of them Linnie, Will, Eda, Ben and Harry; all in their teens except Harry, and he as brave and eager for fun as the others.

After the provisions, bedding, tent and *etceteras* were packed in the wagon it did not look as if there was room for the living portion of the load, but when we safely *stowed* away we had comfortable seats. . . .

After a good lunch we started on and in a short time were among the gigantic redwoods. Words give but a faint idea of the appearance of these grand old monarchs of the forest, so large and tall and straight, tapering gradually to the far away tops. We were all quite excited and looked out first on one side and then on the other, and every few minutes the boys would jump out and measure a tree, until they found one that was over forty feet in circumference and even then they were not satisfied, but wanted to measure another one that looked a little larger.

It was now cool and pleasant, and we soon began to go down, down the mountain, whirling around short turns and still seeing the road winding back and forth below us. There were places which made me feel dizzy to look down, and if the other members of the party had not reminded me of the fact that they were clinging to me I would have been more frightened.

The road was very steep and they kept the brake on the wheels until I became alarmed and said, "Oh, I am afraid the brake will break."

"If it don't brake we shall all be killed," replied the driver coolly.

Occasionally we passed a house built of *shakes,* and in comparison with the trees around, it looked like a playhouse built by some child.

It was nearly sundown when we reached the bottom of the grade at a place called Low Gap, where we were granted permission to camp near the spring on condition that the boys would not shoot the quail, which were so tame that they came up to eat with the chickens.

Low Gap was a very dismal place, dense woods on every side, and as darkness settled around us the girls became somewhat afraid and talked in lugubrious tones of grizzly bears, mountain lions and other beasts of prey. . . .

We had a lively time in the morning, for the pigs smelled our breakfast, and came flocking in from all directions, determined to share it with us, and we were glad when we were ready to resume our upward way.

Now we began to really enjoy our journey, for the air was cool and filled with a woody fragrance that was pleasant and refreshing. The joyous birds welcomed us with their sweetest music, and the bright jay-bird flitted noisily through the trees and ever and anon large flocks of quail would go whirring beyond the reach of a stray shot, while all the time busy squirrels went scampering up the trees, scolding loudly at our intrusion, and the scenery was both beautiful and grand all that day. . . .

We came to a good camping place as the sun was sinking among the distant trees. . . .

. . . Standing where we were and looking down, far down on the tops of the trees, they seemed all on a level, but beyond the canyon the trunks of the massive redwoods and pines were visible from the roots to the branches. What an army of monsters, standing every one a little higher than its nearest neighbor below, and nodding their lofty heads to the ocean wind that marched along the high land but did not dare venture down into the deep gulches; they almost seemed like a battalion of giant soldiers climbing the mountain.

Far above and overhanging the valley, were huge pinnacles of rock which reminded us of ancient castles, with high walls, domes and vestibules, all brilliantly lighted by the fire-rays of the setting sun. While just above the castellated rocks a bright cloud moved silently like a chariot of the heavens, from which we could imagine angels were looking out in order to get a passing glimpse of earth's attractive beauty and thrilling sublimity.

But our pleasant reverie was broken by the shouts of the girls and the crackling of the camp-fire which recalled us to the fact that supper must be prepared. The boys were seen coming through the trees bringing gray squirrels and a young rabbit as their addition to the bill of fare, and the dutch-oven, frying-pan and coffee-boiler were placed over the fire, and a good supply for all was soon ready. . . .

Mendocino City

The next morning we passed an old logging camp. Ben and Harry said they would like to live there all the time, they could have such fun playing on the stumps.

The fire had swept over the fallen trees and the side of the mountain was seamed and scarred where they had sent the huge logs crashing down into the stream. We thought of the grand and beautiful forest through which we had been passing and the contrast between that and this blackened and devastated scene was so great that it made us think of Eden before and after the fall, and we wondered why it was that man so often marred the handiwork of God.

For quite a number of miles our road lay through this despoiled forest. We then entered a damp, dark canyon, so cold we hastily donned our heavy cloaks and coats, and wrapped up in blankets to keep comfortable, while far above our heads the grey light faintly glimmered through the interlaced branches. On one side of the road there was a stream so sluggish that it had formed in pools bordered by coarse sedges.

It was so cold and gloomy that even the birds did not sound a note of praise, although we saw them occasionally flitting from bough to bough and darting across the road before us. An audacious little chipmunk was the only thing that dared make a noise. From the branches which overhung the slimy pools drooped long loops and pendants of ragged grey moss which gave a weird look to the dreary scene, while away through the dark vistas of the forest we imagined we could discover under the mistletoe-crowned oaks just such places as the ancient Druids would have chosen for their most inhuman rites. . . .

We soon came to a large plain that some time in the past had been swept by the fire. Scattered over it here and there were the bare, lifeless trunks of blackened trees. The ground was covered with dark green bushes, which caused one of the company to say, "That looks very much like a blueberry bog;" and as we reached the bushes another exclaimed, "Blueberries! Blueberries!"

The bushes were loaded with berries, and as it was the first time we had seen any growing since we left New England, we went to gathering the fruit, and when we had eaten all we wanted, we filled pails, pans and everything available with the delicious berries.

What a hearty laugh we had after we gathered at the wagon, for we were an exceedingly *blue* looking company. As there was no water on the plain we were obliged to be resigned to our *blue* looks, but we thought if we should meet any one he would conclude water must have been very scarce where we last camped.

The scenery was different now, for we had left the mountains. The trees were not so large and we found hazel and blackberry bushes, but we were too late to share in the nuts and berries. We saw a peculiar looking bush with the nuts growing each in a shell by itself, but about twenty clustered together in a compact ball. They were not quite ripe and we could never learn what they were.

We were very much interested in the different flowers, shrubs and trees and would have lingered longer had we not heard the distant roar of the ocean. As we drew near the coast, expectation was at its height. We all eagerly desired to look out on the rolling billows of the mighty Pacific. The young people clapped their hands and talked and laughed so heartily that a gentle rebuke from the more sedate was occasionally necessary.

But how exceedingly cold and damp it was! Never before had we experienced such a chilling sensation in the month of

July. The fog became so dense that we could see but a few feet in either direction, and the great drops of water fell so constantly from the trees that we almost imagined ourselves in an eastern forest during a shower. But there was something pleasant in the sound of the patter, patter of those drops falling on our wagon-cover from the tops of the trees. The road soon became muddy with pools of water standing here and there, while the horses were as wet as if they had been out in an actual shower, and we were so wrapped in blankets that Ben thought every person we met would think we were traveling mummies. . . .

. . . We found it necessary to obtain another supply of provisions, for the pure mountain air and the cold sea breeze proved to be wonderful tonics. Never once in all the time we were camping did I hear one of the company complain of having no appetite.

One of our number was dyspeptic. Before leaving home he ate but twice a day, and only crackers, broth, rice, or such light articles of diet usually recommended to invalids. Now he ate three hearty meals consisting of coffee, bacon, hot biscuits and wild game, besides vegetables and fruit.

We bought some delicious honey in the comb, and as it was considerable trouble to pack it safely away, Eda volunteered to hold it. The box leaked, and before we reached our camping ground she was as sweet as she had been blue a few hours before. She took the laughter and joking quite coolly, and said: "Now if I hadn't washed off the blue-berries I should have been pretty good sauce." She received immediate assurances that she was saucy enough as it was. . . .

We camped near a pretty little cove and went to bed early, for a gentleman told us it would be low tide about six o'clock in the morning, and a good time to gather abalones.

The roar of the ocean wind and the loud and continuous booming of the waves against the rocky coast were so different from the pleasant music of the forest, which had so long acted as a lullaby in soothing us to rest, that we found it almost impossible to sleep. . . .

Treasures of the Deep

In the morning we found that the ocean had not lifted her veil, but we did not fret about that, for we were determined to remain at the coast until we could have a good view of the Pacific.

We did not wait for breakfast but made ready to go hunting abalones. When the gentleman came along with an iron rod, and a sack, he said if we would go with him he would show us the best place to find them. He led the way along the cliff and finally began to descend an almost perpendicular path. It looked as if it was a perilous undertaking, but the boys and girls went ahead and told me if I fell I could fall on them so I would be all right.

For some distance the path wound under trailing vines, so dense we could not part them, and so low we could not stand erect. When we came to the ledge we found crevices in it which enabled us to cling with more safety, but it was so damp with the ocean spray that we had to "make haste slowly."

The rocks left bare by the tide were covered with sea-moss and weeds. The gentleman lifted some of it and pointing to something beneath said, "That is an abalone." We had never seen an abalone, and the object to which he called our attention looked to us like a bulge in the rock covered with a greyish looking moss, but he inserted his rod at one edge and in a moment more it fell upon the sand. Then the girls said, "Ugh! who could eat such a horrid black thing as that?"

The boys gathered about a dozen, then we went to the camp to have our breakfast. They dug the abalone out of the shells and trimmed off the outside until it could hardly be distinguished from a peeled white turnip; then it had to be sliced and beaten like a piece of tough steak, and fried in hot lard. The children liked them very well, but we never ate anything that had the least resemblance in taste to an abalone. . . .

When the tide was in so we could not go down the cliffs to the rocks we visited the little sheltered cove, where we never tired of watching the billows as they came gently gliding up to the beach, one after the other like children at play.

We found a species of kelp with a turnip-shaped bulb, and a root from one to twenty feet long. The boys considered them a good substitute for whips and had a lively time chasing each other up and down the beach. There was quite a variety of shells, and the girls gathered more than we had room to carry. . . .

All along the cliff we noticed that the pines were very different from those we had passed in the seclusion of the forest. Here, instead of being tall and massive and symmetrical, we found them stunted, dwarfed and gnarled. Continually shaken and beaten by the mighty ocean wind, they leaned toward the mountains, and with their branches all extending in the same direction, they seemed to implore assistance from their sheltered and more favored brethren.

⌣⌣

Mrs. Jacob Barzilla Rideout *lived in San Francisco and was the author of* Six Years on the Border *and* Camping Out in California.

Night Beach

VIC COCCIMIGLIO

I could just as easily be nine years old,
sitting on this beach at high noon,
waiting for my father to swim out to the buoy
and back; but here, neither child nor father,

I am alone, counting my breaths,
thinking about how my grandfather
used to count ants on the patio
while chanting: *I never kill them;*
I never destroy them. Let them live.

If he were still alive
he could be here with me,
and together we could count sandpipers
scuttling along the shore,
now that a new day is forming
as it must have
one hundred million years before we were born.

Born and raised in Pittsburgh, Pennsylvania, **Vic Coccimiglio** *now lives in southern California. His poetry has appeared in numerous magazines and anthologies, including* The Invisible Ladder *(Henry Holt, 1996),* Looking for Your Name *(Orchard Books, 1993), and* Strings: A Gathering of Family Poems *(Bradbury/MacMillan, 1984).*

The Earth Dragon

FROM THE
NORTHERN CALIFORNIA COAST INDIANS

American Indians inhabited the California Coast for thousands of years before the arrival of European settlers. Many tribes were wiped out by disease or lost their homes after Europeans arrived. And many lost the stories and traditions that helped define their culture. All that is known of this story is that it comes from native peoples of the northern California Coast.

Before this world was formed, there was another world with a sky made of sandstone rock. Two gods, Thunder and Nagaicho, saw that old sky being shaken by thunder.

"The rock is old," they said. "We'll fix it by stretching it above, far to the east."

They stretched the sandstone, walking on the sky to do it, and under each of the sky's four corners they set a great rock to hold it up. Then they added the different things that would make the world pleasant for people to live in. In the south they created flowers. In the east they put clouds so that people wouldn't get headaches from the sun's glare. To form the clouds they built a fire, then opened a large hole in the sky so that the clouds could come through. In the west they made another opening for the fog to drift in from the ocean.

Now the two gods were ready to create people. They made a

man out of earth and put grass inside him to form his stomach. They used another bundle of grass for his heart, round pieces of clay for the liver and kidneys, and a reed for the windpipe. They pulverized red stone and mixed it with water to form his blood. After putting together man's parts, they took one of his legs, split it, and turned it into a woman. Then they made a sun to travel by day and a moon to travel by night.

But the creations of the gods did not endure, for every day and every night it rained. All the people slept. Floodwaters came, and great stretches of land disappeared. The waters of the oceans flowed together; animals of all kinds drowned. Then the waters completely joined, and there were no more fields or mountains or rocks, only water. There were no trees or grass, no fish or land animals or birds. Human beings and animals all had been washed away.

The wind no longer blew through the portals of the world, nor was there snow, or frost, or rain. It did not thunder or lightning, since there were no trees to be struck. There were neither clouds nor fog, nor did the sun shine. It was very dark.

Then the earth dragon, with its great, long horns, got up and walked down from the north. It traveled underground, and the god Nagaicho rode on its head. As it walked along through the ocean depths, the water outside rose to the level of its shoulders. When it came to shallower places it turned its head upward, and because of this there is a ridge near the coast in the north upon which the waves break. When it came to the middle of the world, in the east under the rising sun, it looked up again, which created a large island near the coast. Far away to the south it continued looking up and made a great mountain range.

In the south the dragon lay down, and Nagaicho placed its

head as it should be and spread gray-colored clay between its eyes and on each horn. He covered the clay with a layer of reeds, then spread another layer of clay. On it he put some small stones, and then set blue grass, brush, and trees in the clay.

"I have finished," he said. "Let there be mountain peaks on the earth's head. Let the waves of the sea break against them."

The mountains appeared, and brush sprang up on them. The small stones he had placed on earth's head became large, and the head itself was buried from sight.

Now people appeared, people who had animal names. (Later when Indians came to live on the earth, these "first people" were changed into their animal namesakes.) Seal, Sea Lion, and Grizzly Bear built a dance house. One woman by the name of Whale was fat, and that is why there are so many stout Indian women today.

The god Nagaicho caused different sea foods to grow in the water so that the people would have things to eat. He created seaweed, abalones, mussels, and many other things. Then he made salt from ocean foam. He caused the water of the ocean to rise up in waves and said that the ocean would always behave that way. He arranged for old whales to float ashore so that people would have them to eat.

He made redwoods and other trees grow on the tail of the great dragon, which lay to the north. He carved out creeks by dragging his foot through the earth so that people would have good fresh water to drink. He created many oak trees to provide acorns to eat. He traveled all over the earth making it a comfortable place for men.

After he had finished, he and his dog went walking to see how the new things looked. When they arrived back at their starting point in the north, he said to his dog: "We're close to home. Now we'll stay here."

So he left this world where people live, and now he inhabits the north.

This story was recorded in fragments by E. W. Gifford in the 1930s and later published in this form in American Indian Myths and Legends, *edited by Richard Erdoes and Alfonso Ortiz.*

At Sea Ranch Beach

CHERISE WYNEKEN

Purple ice plants
    creep across the cliff,
chartreuse moss
    beards the gray green rock,
golden poppies
    cling along the drop
    over seeping water.
A tangle of dry sea drift
    masses in the cove,
seaweed intestines
    coil driftwood bones,
tasseled trimmings mirror
    necklaces and earrings,
washed white wood
    a loaf of bread,
log dragon
    bares his teeth and growls.

Wielding sticks and clubs,
    we beat on timber bits
syncopating rhythm
    with waves and hands and wood.

Cherise Wyneken *is retired from teaching and raising four children. She lives with her husband in Ft. Lauderdale, Florida, and enjoys sharing her thoughts and experiences with readers through her stories, articles, and poetry. Her collection of poems,* Seeded Puffs, *has been published by Dry Bones Press.*

Fire in the Chaparral!

GRETCHEN WOELFLE AND
CLEA WOELFLE-ERSKINE

Every autumn, fires claim homes and other property in the coastal mountains of California, so it's not surprising that many people view fire as a threat. But by looking closely at the role of fire in chaparral communities, one begins to appreciate that it isn't simply a destructive force.

Day One: Fire!

The sun is about to rise this autumn day, over the steep hills and valleys of southern California's coastal mountains. A hawk takes off from her perch on a live oak tree. She catches a rising thermal current and circles higher and higher, soaring over a patchwork landscape of tall grass, live oak trees, and dense shrubs, called chaparral. Hawk's keen eyes spot a movement in the grass. She swoops down and snatches a ground squirrel for her breakfast.

A mule deer awakens in the grass and walks to the oak grove to browse for acorns. A lizard crawls out of a crack in a boulder as the sun bursts over the mountains.

It has been forty years since the last fire. The chaparral shrubs, some as tall as eight feet, have grown so thick that deer cannot make his way through them, and hawk cannot see into them. But small animals like mice, ground squirrels, rabbits,

snakes, and small birds run beneath
the interlaced branches. All night,
Santa Ana winds have been building
in the Sierra Nevada to the east. As the
sun rises, the hot winds sweep westward
across the desert and into the coastal mountains, all the way
to the Pacific Ocean.

 Miles away, someone throws a cigarette into the dry grass.
The wind takes that smoldering bit of paper and whips it into
a flame. The fire runs through the grass toward some oak
trees. Flames crackle in the brush beneath the trees, leap up to

singe the lower leaves, and catch hold of dead branches in the canopy of the tree.

Then the fire strikes the shrubs. First to burn are dead branches of manzanita and toyon bushes still standing from the last fire. Then the flames consume the living branches of the plants. These branches are filled with oily resin that burns even hotter than the dead wood. The sound of cracking branches grows to a roar, as the fire becomes a firestorm, hurling flaming branches a hundred feet into the air. Clouds of smoke darken the midafternoon sky.

Hawk spies the fire long before it reaches her and she soars away, flying south over a bare peak topped by radio towers. As she crosses the next ridge, she sees a maze of red tile roofs, bright green lawns, and turquoise swimming pools.

Back in the chaparral, lizard feels the heat of the approaching flames. He scurries under a chamise bush into a burrow and disappears underground. As the fire sweeps overhead, the temperature at ground level reaches 1,000 degrees Fahrenheit, hot enough to melt aluminum. Three inches below, temperatures rise to 150 degrees. Lizard burrows a little deeper where the soil is warmed to only 70 degrees. Here animals, roots, and seeds all survive the raging inferno that blazes overhead.

Deer smells the smoke and bounds away. He cannot outrun such a blaze. His only safety lies in the canyon, where willow and sycamore trees line a flowing stream. The fire licks at the tall sycamores, burning leaves and trunks, but then dies down in this damp place. Deer is safe.

Meanwhile, the fire sweeps up and down the mountains, lighting the night sky with an eerie red glow. Toward dawn the Santa Ana wind dies and the fire reaches a stretch of sage and

California buckwheat near the ocean. A damp ocean breeze finally quenches the flames.

Day Two: Blackened Earth

Dawn breaks through a haze of smoke and ash. Smoldering branches of chamise and toyon stand guard as lizard, mouse, and chipmunk emerge from their burrows. They find no food, only blackened earth covered with a crust of resin and soft ash. Lizard leaves a maze of footprints in the ash as he runs down to the stream to hunt for insects.

Deer emerges from the stream bed and sniffs the air. He sees no food on the hillsides, so he walks downstream, browsing on leaves and tender shoots untouched by the fire.

Hawk had to fly three ridges south to escape the fire. As she returns home she sees that the ground cover is gone. A few patches of grass remain unburned, but these do not hide the small creatures from the keen eyes of hawk. After her meal of a rabbit, hawk settles in her favorite oak tree. Dead branches have burned away, but fireproof bark has protected the tree. It will survive and provide a nesting place for hawk.

Fire has always been a part of the life cycle in the chaparral ecosystem. The hunter-gatherer native people in California used fire as a tool to cultivate a comfortable life. Every year they burned the oak groves, which provided them with acorns, their staple food. Acorn moth larvae lived in immature nuts that fell to the ground in summer. The fire burned the acorns and prevented the larvae from hatching into moths and laying more eggs in healthy acorns. Thus fire promoted larger acorn crops and cleared the ground, making harvesting easier.

During the late spring and summer, the tribes gathered

seeds of dozens of species of grasses and wildflowers. Every three to five years, after the seed harvest, the people burned the meadows, choosing a day with no wind and damp air. The whole village drove thousands of grasshoppers into a pit in the center of the field. Then they lit the dry grass. When the fire died down, they feasted on roasted grasshoppers. The ash-fertilized soil produced even bigger seed harvests the following year. Hunting deer, rabbits, and other animals was also easier in the cleared landscape.

Native people let small stands of toyon, manzanita, ceanothus, and other chaparral shrubs grow thick. They ate the manzanita and toyon berries and used other shrubs for firewood, spears, digging sticks, soap, medicine, and fiber. Every ten years they might burn the shrubs, making sure that the areas nearby were cleared. Using fire wisely, the tribes helped to create a landscape that supported a rich diversity of plants and animals.

One Month Later: Winter Rains Arrive

Just a few days after the fire, some shrubs put forth new shoots from an underground root crown, a fat burl that lies deep enough to escape the fire's intense heat. These "crown sprouting" plants are watered by roots as long as forty feet that tap water deep in the earth. But most plant growth comes with the life-giving rain.

One night in late October, storm clouds gather over the mountains. Fat raindrops hit the bare crusted ground and run downhill to fill the stream. Where the rain does penetrate, the ash dissolves into the soil to nourish new plants. Mud slips down the bare hillsides, but the roots of the shrubs hold most of the soil in place.

A few inches down, some seeds have lain dormant since the last fire forty years ago. These "fire-followers" include some species of manzanita and ceanothus shrubs, and certain types of clover and lupine. They need the fire's heat to soften their seed coats and allow water to penetrate. After the rain they burst forth from the blackened soil.

Ripe acorns have dropped from the oak trees. Acorns send long taproots into the wet earth and begin to sprout. Deer finds acorns easily on the bare ground. But mouse and rabbit face a hungry time. They find few seeds to eat and they must forage in the open where they cannot hide from hawk.

The First Spring and Summer: Bountiful Harvests

A riot of grass and wildflowers covers the ground the first spring after the fire. Purple lupine, orange California poppies, rich clover, and monkeyflowers transform the burned landscape into a living carpet of color. During the summer a rich crop of seeds ripens, and all the animals eat well and multiply.

Flying, crawling, and hopping insects feed lizard. Grasses and herbs feed the herbivores like rabbit, mouse, and squirrel. The herbivores feed the carnivores like snake and hawk. Many parts of the landscape feed deer. He munches on oak seedlings and grass, as well as sprouting shrubs.

Down at the stream, the flow of water has slowed to a trickle. New shoots have sprouted from the stump of a burned sycamore tree. A circle of small trees begins to grow where only one giant stood before the fire.

If, at the end of the summer, lightning strikes this mountainside, a fire will not find much fuel—just a light covering of dry grass, dead branches of the burned chaparral, and shoots of the new shrubs. The fire will soon sputter and die.

Five Years Later: The Chaparral Restored

Five years of rain and sun, growth and death have come and gone. The fire-follower plants have vanished, but their seeds lie buried in the soil, waiting for the next fire. Bunch grasses and wildflowers cover the meadows. Scrub oaks, manzanitas, and toyon bushes are growing dense once more. Their branches interlace and hide the ground.

Mouse, lizard, and squirrel forage in these green tunnels. Deer can nibble bark, leaves, and berries only at the edge of the shrubs. Each year that fire does not return, deer has a harder time moving through the grass and around the shrubs. Hawk must work harder too, to see the slight movement that might be her next meal.

Native people recognized that burning the chaparral every few years brought good harvests and easier hunting, and protected the land from devastating fires. Spanish settlers did not understand the role of fire and prohibited the Chumash and Tong-va tribes from burning. Thus, as early as 1826, large areas of unburned chaparral erupted into firestorms. In recent times, more and more people have moved to the hills where the chaparral meets the city. Uncontrolled fires threaten their safety and the health of the ecosystem. When we burn the chaparral in a controlled way, we can decrease the danger to people living in the hills.

By burning the chaparral, we also choose to restore the complex web of life on the steep hills and canyons of the California Coast. Instead of having dense, fire-prone shrubs broken by houses and green lawns, we can bring back the wild slopes of grass and sage, green groves of live oak trees, and deep canyons of willow and sycamore, like those where grizzly bears once roamed.

Fire. Ash. Seeds. Growth. Fuel. Fire. Such is the rhythm of life in the chaparral.

Gretchen Woelfle *lives in Venice, California, close to the Santa Monica Mountains, which burn every few years. She loves to hike in this rich chaparral ecosystem with family and friends, including her daughter, Clea.* **Clea Woelfle-Erskine** *is the author of* The Guerilla Graywater Girl's Guide to Water, *a practical history of water use in the West, and* Water/under/ground, *a zine about natural history and indigenous struggles. She lives in Oakland, California, where she works on land restoration projects with middle-school students.*

Vasquez Rocks

SUE ALEXANDER

Tan-gray slabs of rock,
sandstone boards
that seem pasted
one on another,
tilt up at an angle into
the atmosphere.

Lizards and jackrabbits
scurrying
through the desert canyon
make no sound,
give no hint of
past life lived here.

Not a whisper
of the earthquakes
that formed these rocks
millions of years ago,
nor of the Shoshones
who dwelt in the sand below
amid the manzanita
and juniper.

Not a breath
to tell us of the Spaniards
who came after
and called the canyon
Agua Dulce
for the sweet-water stream
that winters here.

Not an echo
to remind us
of the stagecoach-robbing
bandits
who hid from posses
deep in the shadows
of the slab-formed caves
during the early
California years.

Suddenly,
dust devils sigh
and scutter along the ground
into the caves,

steal grains of sand
and manzanita twigs,
and then disappear.

And I wonder if
(as I am told)
these small swirls of wind
are really the ghosts
of Vasquez
and his gang of desperadoes
who once lived here.

Sue Alexander *is a full-time writer and the author of more than twenty books for young readers including the critically acclaimed* Nadia the Willful *and* Lila on the Landing. *Her fascination with the southern California landscape began when she was a child visiting her grandparents and continued when, as an adult, she moved to a community within Los Angeles. When her three children were young, she and her husband took them on many outings that combined her interest in the history of California with the landscape.*

The Marsh at the Edge of Arcata

DANIELLE JEANNE DROLET

Marshes used to be thought of as mosquito-filled wastelands. Over time, though, we've come to appreciate that these wetlands actually abound with life and act as natural water purifiers. Many cities, including Arcata, California, now celebrate marshes as centerpieces of their communities.

Jill has a new haircut. It's one of those feathered cuts that look great when you're standing at the Arcata Marsh watching a red-tailed hawk circle a field for mice and a warm, spring wind is blowing through your hair.

Jill's my Little. I'm her Big. We were matched by North Coast Big Brothers/Big Sisters more than two years ago. "The marsh"—as most people around here call it—is one of our favorite places to go on an outing.

We bring the binoculars. Sometimes we bring a picnic. We always bring the dogs. They don't mind leashes when delectable smells haunt every inch of the trails that wind around marshes, ponds, and even a small lake. A bright flurry of birds, the deep croak of a frog, other animals passing and leaving their scent—the marsh is full of fascination for the dogs as well as us.

The marsh is located at the edge of the town of Arcata, smack on the California coast. Its official name is the Arcata Marsh and Wildlife Sanctuary. It was completed in 1981 as a way to solve this problem: What does a town do with the tons of wastewater that pour out from each household and business every day?

For many years the wastewater was sent straight to the bay, which leads into the Pacific Ocean. This is harmful to the plant and animal life. Then the town started using chlorine to treat the wastewater. The chlorine cleaned the water, but it poisoned plants and animals.

In the 1970s, a new system was developed. Now the wastewater is treated by a natural process. At the Arcata Marsh, sewage is first sent through the "Headworks" where solids are separated out. The wastewater passes through a series of ponds and six marshes, one after the other. Microorganisms filter and feed on the waste. Marsh plants draw nutrients from the water. Over time, and after more processing, the water is purified, then sent back into the bay.

These marshes are now a safe home, or sanctuary, for thousands of birds, many fish, and other creatures, as well as a wide variety of plants. The marsh system creates a beautiful park, which is also a terrific place for walking dogs, having a picnic ... and showing off a new haircut.

Outings at the marsh for me and Jill also give her the chance to show that her Big Sister doesn't know everything.

The red-tailed hawk has flown off—without a mouse to eat—and we are hiking merrily along a trail when Jill asks me, "Do you know what that is?" She points to a grassy plant growing in some low water.

"Uh ... grass?" I ask.

"No," she says with a little smile. "It's bulrush. It grows in freshwater, like in ponds."

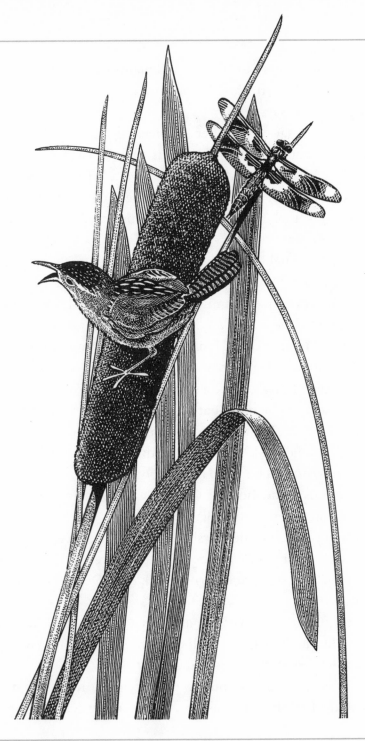

She also points out that the tall plants called cattails, with their velvety brown "tails," grow in water too. "They're called *emergents*," she says.

"Okay," I say, eyeing her suspiciously. How'd she get so smart? I wonder. I know she wants to be a teacher someday. But she's barely ten and appears to be ready for college soon.

Along another path, by the lake, she roughs her hand in a feathery green plant that comes up to my nose. A licorice scent imbues the air.

"That's fennel," she says.

"Funnel? It's named after a kitchen implement?"

She stares at me, unamused. "*Fennel.* It's used in cooking," she says, as if she used it all the time.

"Not in my cooking," I mumble, and we move on.

We come to the new telescope mounted on one side of the trail. I peer through to see a swarm of shorebirds swoop like a roller coaster on wings. Soaring up, diving down, the dunlins flash their white bellies and dip right over our heads.

"Jill," I finally ask, watching the dunlins rise over the mud-flats, "how do you know so much about these plants?"

She runs ahead, holding Cinco's leash. "A man came to our school and told us," she calls into the air.

"Told you about the marsh?" I yell, trying to keep up. I have Moki, the older dog. We're both a little slower.

"Yup." She stops and turns to ask me. "Do you know why they built it?"

"Yes, I do," I say with an air of erudition (which means I sound like a know-it-all). Still catching my breath, I say, "The marsh was created in order to . . ."

"An egret!" Jill cries out. She is, it seems, much less inter-ested in what I have to say than in the snowy egret lifting off from an island in the middle of the lake. The large bird floats in a smooth line over the water. Its perfectly white body is brightened by sunlight and stunning to see. Egrets are great fishers, and Franklin Klopp Lake has lots of fish.

We trot along the trail, trying to follow the egret through the binoculars. We are pounding our feet and panting as we follow the dirt path. Suddenly a blabbering squall of mallards pulls our gaze from the egret to a large pond. Startled by us, the ducks wade away to the pond's bright blue center as fast as ducks can. They move through a thick mass of duckweed—the salad bar of duck dining. Duckweed floats at the water's edge, making a bright green cover, and ducks love it. No ranch dressing needed.

We watch the ducks swim away in one large mass, as if they were a single animal instead of thirty or more. When we turn back to search the sky, the egret is out of sight.

That's how the marsh is. One thing after another grabs your eye, makes you wonder, leaves you stunned.

We decide to stop and eat our lunch on a wooden bench inside a one-room "house" beside the pond. These houses are called observation blinds. Planted here and there along the trails, the blinds have a large open window. We can sit inside, out of the rain if it's raining (which it does a lot around here) and watch the birds. But the birds can't see us.

We munch on potato chips and tuna sandwiches. And we watch. Little birds called marsh wrens flit around in the bushes. Jill even spots one as it climbs to the top of a cattail to sing its pretty song. The dogs lie in the cool shade of the shelter, snagging a fallen chip or two.

After we put all our leftovers into the pack, we decide to

make our last stop of the day at a spot near an old lumber mill called Butcher's Slough. The man who visited Jill's school told her it was called an estuary.

"That's where saltwater from the ocean comes together with freshwater from rivers," she says. "It's like a big pot of soup."

"A pot of what?" I ask, thinking of chicken noodle, maybe minestrone.

"Soup," she says. "For all the animals."

"Oh. You mean they eat the water?"

"No." She is getting impatient with me again. "They eat microscopic animals *in* the soup."

As we come to the slough, we know we might spot the egret again, or even a black-crowned night heron. It's their favorite restaurant. Something white flashes and I think I see the egret when Jill shouts, "Pickleweed!"

I turn to see who she is talking to and find her snapping off a small branch that looks like—yes, pickles!

"Here, taste it," she says, shoving it under my nose.

"No, thanks," I say, backing away. "I just had lunch."

"No. Just taste it," she insists. "You can eat it. It's okay."

I look around, hoping to see the egret, an osprey, maybe even a white-tailed kite—anything to save me from the pickleweed. But the slough is still. I take the stem and nibble a tiny bite.

"Ooh," I say, scrunching my face. "It's salty."

"It has salt in it from the water," Jill explains. "Most plants can't live where it's salty. But pickleweed can. It sweats out the salt."

"Oh! Like a filter?" I ask.

She nods at me, smiling. Finally, I get something right.

The egret seems to have disappeared, but we see a great blue heron land its heavy body in the cordgrass. We laugh as it almost topples to one side. Jill bends a length of cordgrass toward us and shows me how it forms salt crystals on its leaf blades. Thankfully, she doesn't make me eat it.

The air is turning cooler, and the day is at its end. We continue our walk along the slough, back over the little bridge and up the trail to the parking lot where our trek began. The dogs lap water from bowls kept in the back of the car. Jill and I look out over the hill called Mount Trashmore. Under the hill is a big pile of trash. It used to be a dump, but now it's a field of wild grasses. That's where we saw the red-tailed hawk, circling for mice. A soft wind is still blowing. Jill's haircut still looks great. And the afternoon sun is sliding down in the west.

"Well, Jill," I say. "Should we come back again soon?"

"Mm," she mumbles kind of dreamily as she stares out toward the pond and the purpling sky. Then, very softly, she says, "I want to live here."

And I know just what she means.

❧

Danielle Jeanne Drolet *lives with her two dogs and a cat among the redwoods on the coast of northern California. She is a teacher, poet/writer, and a Big Sister to Jillian Miles.*

Reapers and Sowers

In Trees

ROBIN BEEMAN

Redwoods grow only in the so-called fog belt of the California Coast—a narrow belt between five and thirty-five miles inland from the sea. Many of these great trees grow in parks and forest preserves, but others grow in people's yards, where they depend on the protection and care of tree-loving individuals.

In good times I could go somewhere in town and find my father in a tree. John Tree is the name on the door of his old Chevy truck, although his name is really John McIlroy. John Tree, however, is the name to call if your tree is in trouble. My dad loves trees. He only wears spikes when he has to. He has a pair of soft leather shoes that he'd rather use so he doesn't hurt the tree. Since I was eight I could ride my bike to watch him work, to hear him murmur to the branches like the best doctor—explaining, consoling. "Hello, Laurel," he'd call to me when he saw me looking up. Laurel, of course, is also the name of a tree.

Today is Saturday and I'm on my way to check on him in his apartment. I'm supposed to meet my friend Mark after lunch and try out his new mountain bike on the trails behind my house. But I always visit my dad on Saturday mornings now. Weekdays after school I work in a book store, and trying to fit everything in is getting to be difficult, but I can't not visit

my father. After he and my mother separated—it was her idea—
he just stopped doing things.

He blamed it on a fall that happened on a job right after he
moved out; he hadn't used the extra rope. A limb cracked under
his weight and he went crashing through branches to the
ground. Nothing was broken, but he injured his back and he
couldn't use his left leg. He was in traction for two weeks. Mom
felt terrible and blamed herself, but she said she needed her
own life—she couldn't go back. They'd gotten married young.
She hadn't even gone to college. The doctor says if my dad takes
it easy, he can go back to work. But my dad won't leave the
apartment. He sits on the couch drinking coffee and watching
television. Sometimes he doesn't even turn up the sound.

I coast down the hill from our house, round a hairpin corner, and pass Mrs. Duffy's place when I see something that
makes my heart stop. Each of Mrs. Duffy's three giant redwood trees is wearing a bright red plastic ribbon around its
trunk. Red plastic ribbons mean disaster for trees. Mrs. Duffy
is standing under one of them fingering the ribbon. I brake.

"Laurel," she says, running toward me. She reminds me of a
pigeon, broad on top with tiny quick legs. Her eyes are bright
and birdlike too. "Laurel," she repeats and I can see that she's
really upset. "Some men from the county came out early this
morning and condemned my trees. They say they're hazards,
that the tops could snap off in a storm and fall onto the road
down at the bottom of the hill."

"That's crazy," I say. "These trees have been here forever."

"Over on Green Gulch Road, Mr. Grimaldi's tree broke off
and landed on someone's roof. I was thinking of getting your
father, but I never see him anymore."

"He and my mom are separated. He lives in town now."

"Oh," she says and reaches out and pats my hand. I feel bad when I've told her this. I can see it makes her even more distressed. "I'm sorry, dear."

"I'll get him to come by," I say. "I know he can help."

I rap on the door to his apartment. "Dad, it's me."

"I've just been resting," he says when he finally opens it. He's in a T-shirt and old jeans. He hasn't shaved since my last visit when I told him I wasn't going to sit in the same room with a porcupine.

The house smells like old coffee and sadness. "It's a great day," I say. "Autumn used to be your favorite time of year. Remember how you liked to drive me around when the leaves fell off so you could show me the scaffolding of the branches?"

"I remember," he mumbles. He turns his back to me and goes into the kitchen. "You want something to eat? There's tuna and some peanut butter."

"What are you going to do when you run out of food?" I ask, following. "What if I stop shopping for you?"

"Aw, Laurel, don't give me a hard time," he says. His face is gray. The whole room is gray. I pull up a shade. He blinks at the sudden light.

"I've got a job for you."

"I can't work."

"You can do some work. It's old Mrs. Duffy. The county wants her to cut her redwoods, those big beautiful trees. I told her you'd do something."

"Laurel, you shouldn't promise things."

"Take a shower and shave, Dad."

He goes into the bathroom without any protest this time. While he's there, I open all the windows. It's a studio apartment and in a few minutes the cool breezes are rushing through, taking away the tired air. I'm afraid even cool autumn breezes don't do much for the smell of sadness, though, which seems to have sunk deep into everything, into the plaid of the couch and the cracked Naugahyde of the old armchair, into the rust-colored carpeting.

My mother says I shouldn't be helping—that he has to come out of this on his own. She says she knows him better than I do. She believes that she took care of him so well, he never learned to take care of himself—or her.

Surprisingly, his old truck starts right away. Two weeks ago I made him drive us to the big discount grocery to stock up. He's not getting insurance for his back injury anymore so every nickel counts. On the way he's quiet. I know it's hard for him to drive along roads to the place where we all used to live. He pulls up in front of Mrs. Duffy's, and I notice he avoids looking over to where our house sits. He has a long stride normally, a tall man's stride, but now he walks tentatively, like someone who's just gotten off a boat.

Mrs. Duffy must have seen us coming. "John," she says, reaching out with both hands to take his. "It's so good to see you. I can't tell you how glad I am. I know how busy you must be."

"I don't have my equipment with me," he says. "This is just a look-see."

"I understand. I just took some banana bread out of the oven and there's fresh coffee. We really have to have a little visit."

I watch him trying to smile, avoiding her eyes. His eyes are deep set and dark brown and sometimes it's hard to tell where his gaze is. I get a pain in my chest when I see how hard it is for him to be here.

When I was little I named the trees I knew best. I called the big twisted madrone in front of our house Ringo. Every morning my dad would say, "Hi, Ringo," when he walked out to go to work. He knows every tree in the area. He came to California in the Navy and fell in love with them—all of them—the laurels, the maples, the different kinds of oaks, those that lose their leaves once a year and those that shed all the time, like big shaggy pets. And of course, he loves the redwoods that grow in the mountains between our valley and the ocean. He walks to one of the trees and stretches out his hand and places it on the bark. His hand is large, with long fingers. I'm glad for the tree when he touches it.

"Come try this, Laurel," Mrs. Duffy calls. She's in the door with a plate. "Have a taste and tell me what you think." The bread, moist and full of nuts, is delicious and I tell her so. "Some people like it better cold," she says.

"No. Hot, like this," I say, and she nods agreement.

When I go out again, my father is leaning his head against the tree, his back to me. When I walk around I see his face is pale.

"Dad . . ."

"Tell Mrs. Duffy there's nothing I can do."

"Dad, you told me that trees act like sails in the wind. When they get too much wind they snap like a mast. If they get thinned properly, then the wind goes right through them."

"That's all true," he says, and his voice comes out so softly I can barely hear it, "but I can't do it."

"You've done things that are fifty times harder. This is a straight climb. For you it's easy."

"Nothing's easy anymore."

"You're a big baby," I tell him as we drive back. He doesn't answer.

"I sold my equipment."

"That's just an excuse," I say. "Think about the trees. They can't do anything for themselves."

"You're hard, Laurel."

Neither of us says anything until he's back in his driveway. I'm surprised by how angry I am. "I'm tired of feeling sorry for you," I say and jump out of the truck and unload my bike. I refuse to look back as I ride off. I have my tears to protect.

Mark's bike eats up the trail. He follows me on mine. I want to be excited about the bike for his sake. I know how long he's worked for it, but I'm as dismal as the clouds moving in over us. I feel my face muscles work when I try to smile.

Later, we sit on rocks looking down on the town. He holds the bike, turning the gears and admiring them as they turn.

"I love your bike," I say. "It's my father that I'm upset about."

"Is he still hiding out?" Mark tilts his head to study me. His eyes are gray like the sky and concerned. I turn away. I'm not going to let myself cry in front of him.

We take a back path down, riding through golden maple leaves fallen along the creek bank. As we stand on the street corner, leaning on our bikes and saying good-bye, I see my Dad's truck come from the street that leads up to our house. He doesn't look in our direction.

The phone rings almost as soon as I walk in the door. "Laurel," he says. I start to hang up but there's something new—or maybe old—in his voice.

"Listen, Laurel, I need a ground person."

"What do you mean?"

"I need help. Meet me at Mrs. Duffy's in half an hour."

There's a wind from the west and I can smell the ocean on the other side of the ridge. A fine drizzle falls. Winter feels close. When I round the bend I see the pickup parked on the side of the road. There's a figure in a yellow poncho at the base of the tallest redwood.

"I thought you sold your equipment," I say when I get there. He's tossing up a rope. He already has on the harness. By the side of the tree is a canvas pack with tools.

"I called a friend on the other side of the valley and borrowed stuff from him."

"What's going on?"

He looks at me for the first time since I've gotten there. His eyes are still sad, but there's something different in them—a light. The wind is blowing the scent of the trees down to us. His long fingers work the rope through the metal loops of the harness. He plants his right boot with the spike into the fringy bark of the tree. Then the other spike. He leans back and tests the harness. He pulls on the ropes he's slung over the branches above him.

"What?" I ask again.

"I'm going up," he says. I can see that his hands are trembling.

"Dad . . . ," I say. Now I'm worried.

"It's all right," he says, looking up. The wind is making the tops of the trees sway wildly. "It's going to be quite a ride. When I get there, I want you to send up the pack."

"Are you sure you want to do this?"

"Did you know that a tree acts like a sail in the wind, but if it's properly thinned the wind can go through it?"

I smile and nod. "You told me that once."

"I did? Well, when I've thinned these trees, I think I can convince the county that they should stay. I don't want to lose them. They have names, you know."

"They do, don't they," I say. "I knew you'd name them." This time I think the light in his eyes is a tear, but then the wind is fierce. I wipe my own eyes.

He starts up. I know he's shaking a little under the poncho. I'm shaking too. Up he goes. Through the spokes of limbs, higher and higher.

"What are their names?" I call when he's reached the top, but the wind is whipping the trees so much that he can't hear me. He spreads out his arms and the poncho billows behind him like a bright wing, but I know he won't fly off. I know we're both where we want to be.

$\smile$

Robin Beeman *grew up in Louisiana, studied and taught in Mexico, and now lives in the hills of northern California. She has published stories, essays, and reviews in many venues. Her books are* Parallel Life and Other Stories *and* A Minus Tide, *her new book is* The Lost Art of Desire *(2001). "In Trees" was a 1990 PEN Syndicated Fiction winner.*

Plum Trees

ALISON SEEVAK

There are no seasons in California,
just two plum trees
in my backyard.
All winter,
bare and knotted
like my mother's hands,
nails unpolished,
no wedding band.
In spring,
they bloom into
teenaged girls
who pull snowy slips
over their heads.
They are the daughters I may never have.
Come June,
they throw temper tantrums,
toss ripe, purple fruit
to the ground.
I don't mind.
I pick up after them,
an exasperated housewife
gathering strewn, dirty clothes
for another load of laundry,

but humming
all the while.
Later,
I turn the shiny pages of magazines,
tear out recipes
for pudding,
tortes,
jam.
Anything,
I think,
anything
to make good use
of plums.

〜✎

Alison Seevak *is a poet and teacher whose writing has appeared in anthologies and literary journals including the* Sun, Lilith, *and* Many Mountains Moving. *Born in Boston and raised in New Jersey, she has lived in the San Francisco Bay Area for more than ten years.*

Catalina's Pigeon Express

RICHARD BAUMAN

Santa Catalina is the third largest of the eight Channel Islands and the only one with a resident human population. Sunny for an average of 267 days a year, Catalina has long attracted vacationers. And many years ago, it attracted a most unusual business.

Even before the invention of the airplane, a unique kind of air-mail service was in full swing between Santa Catalina Island and Los Angeles on the California mainland.

In 1894, Catalina was an island mecca for the social elite. Wealthy people from all over California called the island home between June and September every year. They could be found sunning themselves on Catalina's beaches, sipping cocktails on pleasure boats anchored in Avalon Harbor, playing golf, or partaking of other resort activities.

While island access was reasonably easy via the steamship *Hermosa,* rapid communication between island and mainland was another matter. The radio hadn't yet been invented, and neither telegraph nor telephone cable spanned the channel. If there was desperate need to contact Los Angeles from Catalina, or vice versa, it took a boat several hours to travel the twenty-five-mile San Pedro Channel.

Some vacationers relished Catalina's isolation. On the other hand, those trying to keep tabs on the stock market, their businesses, or world affairs weren't thrilled with such seclusion.

Then along came Otto Zahn with his radical idea of starting an airmail service—the Pigeon Express.

Zahn owned seventy-five homing pigeons that he could train to fly messages back and forth between Avalon and Los Angeles. As bizarre as the idea sounds, it was a viable concept.

Knowing that the Western Union Telegraph Company had no intentions of connecting its services to Catalina in the foreseeable future, Otto met with Hancock Banning, then owner of Catalina Island. Banning agreed to build Otto an office and pigeon loft on the wharf at Avalon. In return, Otto would train his pigeons to fly from Los Angeles to Catalina and back again, carrying messages both ways.

When Otto arrived on Catalina on 12 July 1894 with dozens of trained pigeons in cages, he was greeted by hundreds of vacationers eager to send messages home.

The Pigeon Express fascinated nearly everyone. Otto was inundated with questions as he handed out fliers about his airmail service. "There will be two scheduled flights a day," he said. "I will use no less than two pigeons per flight, and as many as four, depending on how many messages there are."

How much did it cost to send a message on the Pigeon Express? There were two prices. Messages sent on morning flights cost a dollar each. Missives flying in the afternoon traveled for just fifty cents. Afternoon flights cost less because they were subsidized by the *Los Angeles Times,* which had hired Otto's pigeons to fly dispatches of social news from Avalon to Los Angeles during the vacation season.

Dispatches had to be penned on special, ultralight onionskin forms that were three and three-fourths inches by two and one-half inches. There was no limit on the number of words, but each form constituted a single message. The onionskin forms were folded lengthwise into half-inch-wide strips, then wrapped around a pigeon's legs and tied in place. One bird could carry twenty to thirty messages.

Zahn had planned to use just two birds on the inaugural flight, but nearly everybody in Avalon wanted to send a message to the mainland. He added two more birds to meet customer demand.

Zahn's favorite pigeon, Orlando, was leader of the first flight. Even though it was a gray, overcast morning, all of Avalon stood shivering at dockside, eager to witness the maiden flight of the Pigeon Express.

When Otto released his pigeons, they circled Avalon once, flying several hundred feet above the town. Then they abruptly turned toward Los Angeles and disappeared into the gray, overcast morning.

In Los Angeles, Oswald Zahn, one of Otto's brothers, kept a nervous vigil, peering into the mist, hoping for a glimpse of Orlando and the other birds. It was nearly 10:30 A.M., and Oswald reckoned the pigeons should be swooping into the loft within a minute or two.

Had Oswald been a nail-biter, he would have chewed off his fingertips waiting. The clock struck 11:00 A.M., and the loft was still bare. If Otto had launched the birds as scheduled at 9:30, they should have landed by now.

Oswald reassured himself by reminding Lorenzo, his younger brother, that Orlando was smart and resourceful. "He probably flew above the overcast," Oswald explained again and again, "so he could find his way home."

A few minutes after 11:00, a bell rang in the loft. Orlando had arrived! A couple of minutes later, the other birds flew in, ringing the bell and registering their arrival times. Heavy clouds and fog had slowed them down, obscuring the landmarks they relied on for navigation.

Oswald and Lorenzo quickly unwrapped and sorted the messages. Two had out-of-town destinations and were telegraphed to their recipients. The other message slips were put into envelopes, which Lorenzo delivered by bicycle.

As guests on Catalina settled into a routine of sending messages, Otto followed an unwavering system. He collected his "airmail" from a special box in front of Catalina's premier hotel. He wrapped messages around the legs of his pigeons and sent them heading for Los Angeles exactly on schedule.

Most of the messages were nothing but social banter, but occasionally the pigeons were used for emergency flights. It took a boat at least three hours to make the trip to the mainland, while a pigeon could cover the distance in less than an hour.

Pigeons were used to summon doctors in emergency situations. One time a bird even called the police to Catalina. A wanted man was spotted operating Avalon's target-shooting concession. Deputy sheriffs hurried to the island and easily arrested the ne'er-do-well.

The Pigeon Express operated between Catalina and Los Angeles until 1898. While the birds were faster at crossing the channel than steamships and private boats, they couldn't outrace radio waves. Guglielmo Marconi's invention of the wireless ultimately grounded the Pigeon Express. But during its heyday, when Otto Zahn's airmail service made several hundred flights across the channel, his pigeons never failed to reach their destination.

Richard Bauman *is a writer from West Covina, California, who enjoys history and writing about it. His articles have appeared in scores of national magazines. He is the author of the day-by-day calendar,* "Legal Lunacies." *He recently published his first book,* Awe-full Moments: Spirituality in the Commonplace.

The Lost Hills

MITALI PERKINS

The Santa Monica Mountains are part of California's Transverse Range, east-west running hills and peaks that also include the Santa Ynez and San Gabriel Mountains. Once covered with oak woodlands and shrubs, the lower slopes of many of these mountains are increasingly being cleared to create more living space for the region's growing human population.

I let Strider off the leash and he runs ahead, disappearing into the early morning mist. The hills are quiet, as if they're still sleeping under the covers and don't want to face the day. The trucks haven't started their roaring, dumping, and digging. I'm glad the mist is hiding the brown scar they've already cut across the curves of the lowest green slopes.

My retriever and I have taken early morning hikes in the Santa Monica Mountains since I was nine years old. At first my parents didn't want me to go out alone. This is Los Angeles, after all. Freeway shootings and murders are in the news almost every day. My parents worry that I'll become another item in the daily crime report. I'd probably get a lot of press coverage. "Thirteen-Year-Old Girl's Body Found in Foothills." Just the kind of scandal to make people stop channel surfing and tune in.

Finally Mom and Dad realized that a kid who gets really nervous in crowds and hates talking to strangers needs tons of time alone. When I was in third grade, I'd come home with migraines after all the noise and fuss at school. The only thing that stopped the headaches was storing up an hour's worth of silence in the morning. Dad made me take his cell phone along, and Strider and I would set off into the open land behind our house.

I like to leave before sunrise if I can. Like today, when the light is slowly getting brighter around me. I take deep breaths and inhale the smells of sweet mint, spicy sage, and California lilac. The fragrant, spiky bushes and prickly scrub crowd the trail, but I'm wearing jeans and tennis shoes, so I don't mind.

A pair of chipmunks darts across the path, and I call Strider back before he can chase them. He comes slowly but cheerfully, sniffing the air and low bushes as if he can't get enough of them.

"Heel," I tell him, keeping my voice low. "Good boy."

The trail passes a single, stately live oak with tangled branches that reach high into the mist. I stop and greet the ancient tree like I always do, and a woodpecker answers, knocking somewhere high above my head. A group of sage sparrows adds a soft, tinkling song, and I know that somewhere behind the mist the sun must have risen. I listen with one hand against the rough, dry bark, gathering the strength I'll need to survive the speech I have to make in Social Studies class.

After a while, I start walking again and pass the place where the trucks stand idle. The grass seems tired, heavy with dust from the construction. The trail goes on beyond where they're building, and I climb until I reach a peak high above the mist. Standing in the sunshine, I glimpse a silver strip of ocean behind the acres of low, rolling sagebrush-covered hills. Strider sits on his haunches beside me, panting as he surveys the view. A large green field slopes down from our feet to meet the rise of the next hill.

In a few weeks, this whole place will be covered with wild-flowers. On sunny Saturdays, I'll bring my sketchbook and draw golden California poppies sprinkled in a sea of purple lupine. In a year or so, though, the field of poppies and lupine will be gone, replaced by a manicured lawn and a sprinkler system. Some family living in a gated neighborhood will enjoy my view from their six-bedroom home. I won't be able to get near it.

Today we only have time for a quick look before we have to turn back. I still have to eat breakfast before I catch the school bus. "Let's go, boy," I say, and Strider takes off down the hill toward home.

I take longer steps, trying to catch up with him, bounding down the slope to where the mist is still clinging. I shouldn't have let him off-leash. It's almost time for the rattlesnakes to come out from their winter hiding places.

"Strider!" I call, but there's no sign of him in the mist.

Then I see the shadowy shape poised on the trail below. It's too small to be my dog. A gust of wind pushes away the mist, and a gray fox stands motionless in the pale sunshine. He turns his head, and our eyes lock. The hair along his back bristles. He's thin, I notice. Very thin. My dog barks on the trail beyond him. Quickly, gracefully, the fox leaps into the sagebrush. I grab Strider, put him back on-leash, and watch the fox lope down the canyon. Every fifty yards or so, he turns to see if I am coming too.

Foxes usually roam in the night and sleep in the day. It's early springtime, though, and all the animals are looking for mates. I wonder if he's been searching all night. Now he's heading away from the construction, but there's nowhere for him to go in that direction. He'll hit the freeway soon. I hope there's a female fox on this side of the road. If not, he'll try to cross eight busy lanes to reach the state park on the other side.

I take one last look at the quiet, unprotected hills beyond

the new housing development. If only I could take out Dad's cell phone and dial an emergency number. "Help!" I'd say. "I'm losing my hills, and a fox is heading for trouble!" But I don't know anybody to call.

Maybe someday I'll invent a job where people like me are waiting on the other end of the phone. Another shy kid who desperately needs her quiet morning walk will call. "They're tearing up the hills," she'll tell me. "The animals have nowhere to go." I make my promise to the hills, to the fox, to the solitary walkers in the Santa Monica Mountains: I'll do everything I can to keep you safe.

﹀ ﹀

Mitali Perkins *was born in India and is a Bengali American. She became a California girl soon after she immigrated, attending Stanford and the University of California-Berkeley because she wanted to stay near the California hills. She and her husband have twin boys, James and Timothy, and a Labrador retriever named Strider. She is the author of* The Sunita Experiment *(Little, Brown and Company).*

In the New Garden

A Cantonese Rhyme from San Francisco Chinatown

TRANSLATED BY MARLON K. HOM

Beginning in the years of the Gold Rush, large numbers of Cantonese immigrants arrived in America, which they called "Gold Mountain" because of its promised riches. San Francisco's Chinatown soon became a center for Cantonese life and culture. This rhyme, one of 1,640 folk rhymes published in a set of anthologies called Songs of Gold Mountain, *reflects some of the responses of an anonymous Chinatown poet to his new homeland.*

A cool breeze, a warm day,
A leisurely walk around the New Garden.*
Willows green, peaches red, all are marvelous sights;
I don't mind the fragrant paths leading a distance away.
All the more delighted,
I wander along, to the east, to the west.
Each blade of grass and every blooming flower can cheer a
troubled mind.
O, why not take it easy and enjoy everything all over again?

* *"New Garden"—a term for Golden Gate Park used by the Chinese in San Francisco during the 1900s.*

Marlon K. Hom *is a professor of Asian American Studies at San Francisco State University.*

To Catch a Grunion

AILEEN KILGORE HENDERSON

Most people who plan to catch a fish reach for a line, a hook, and some bait. But if you want to catch grunion on the California coast, the only thing to reach for is . . . a grunion!

⌣

Spring along the southern California coast has a different meaning from spring any place else in the world. That's because the grunion start running. Sometime in March, depending on when the spring high tide will be, the newspapers will headline: "Grunion Run Tonight." The article tells the exact time the run is expected, usually beginning about eleven P.M., and the beach where it will happen. People of all ages rush to get together their swimsuits, jackets, boots, buckets, and flashlights. They make sure they're on the beach ahead of time. Facing the ocean, they watch silently as Orion dips down toward the horizon, and wait for the grunion.

First, the scouts come leaping out of the incoming tide, small male fish with silver sides. If the people watching keep quiet and don't shine their lights, the scouts communicate to the thousands of fish like themselves waiting offshore that the beach is safe. And in come the others on the exact right wave— not the one that washes farthest up on the beach, but the one that follows it—a writhing horde of eight-inch-long silver bodies crowding upon the shore. They appear to be dancing and frolicking, but their purpose is serious.

The strange sight triggers screams and shouts from the people. They snap on their lights and jump about among the fish, trying to catch them. The noise and lights don't matter now—once a grunion run starts, nothing can stop it. The lights reveal the largest of the grunion, the females, digging their tails into the sand with a side-to-side motion that buries half their bodies. Then they begin a front-to-back nodding that signals to the males that the egg laying has begun. While a female deposits up to three thousand pale pink eggs deep in the sand, one or more male grunion leap to encircle her. The males release milt, which soaks through the sand to fertilize the eggs.

The ritual is completed in a minute or less. Those fish that escape the grasping hands of the grunion hunters ride the

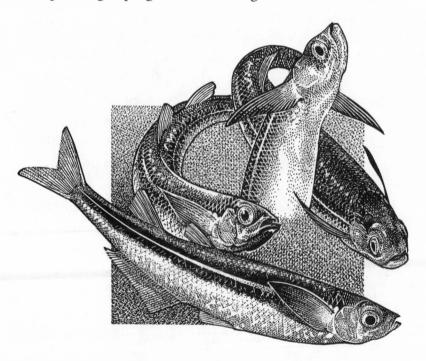

next wave back to sea. There they wait for the second high tide later in the month, and the grunion run is repeated on a different beach.

Meanwhile the eggs under the sand are developing into young grunion. In ten days or two weeks, when the next high tide uncovers their hiding places, they are ready. In one minute they hatch, popping out of the egg case like popcorn, as one grunion authority describes it. Then the wave pulls them out to sea and they begin growing into adults. Next spring they will ride the waves in to a southern California beach to spawn, and so carry on life for their species.

By the time the grunion run is over, Orion has set beyond the western edge of the ocean. The wet, chilled grunion hunters collect their pails of fish and straggle home. After cleaning them, most people roll the fish in cornmeal and fry them for a tasty breakfast. The law does not limit the number of fish taken, but it does forbid taking more than you can use. Also grunion can be taken only with the bare hands, and that is not so easily done. At the height of the spawning season—April and May—harvesting grunion is not allowed.

Spring in southern California is a time for celebrating a unique after-dark event that combines the awesome with the appetite—the running of the grunion.

~ ~

Aileen Kilgore Henderson is an educator and a freelance writer with B.S. and M.A. degrees from the University of Alabama. She has taught school in Alabama, Texas, and Minnesota. Her stories and articles have appeared in Sierra, Odyssey, and other magazines, and she has published three middle-grade novels.

Aparición

GABRIEL TRUJILLO MUÑOZ

Como las ballenas
Que cruzan el océano
En los meses de invierno
En la página en blanco
Las palabras emergen

Uno las observa
Sin entender qué milagro
Pudo hacerlas visibles

Sin comprender
A qué se debe
Compartir con ellas
Semejante privilegio

Tal vez las palabras emergen
Para tomar un poco de aire
Antes de continuar su travesía
O para manifestarle al mundo
Su gozo y su contento

Como las ballenas
Que cruzan el océano
En los meses de invierno

Apparition

Like the whales
That cross the ocean
In the winter months
Words emerge
On the blank page

One observes them
Without understanding what miracle
Could have made them visible

Without comprehending
The reason
For sharing
Such a privilege

Perhaps the words surface
To take a little air
Before continuing their voyage
Or to manifest to the world
Their joy and happiness

Like the whales
That cross the ocean
In the winter months

Gabriel Trujillo Muñoz *is coeditor of the literary magazine* Trazadura *and a founding editor of the Binational Press. He works in the Office of Academic Affairs of the Autonomous University of Baja California.*

The Lone Woman of San Nicolas Island

Helen Foster James

Anyone who has read Scott O'Dell's novel Island of the Blue Dolphins *knows something about the woman who lived alone on San Nicolas Island for eighteen years. O'Dell chose to fictionalize his account, but in this essay Helen Foster James shares the recorded details of the real lone woman's life.*

In 1835, eighteen native inhabitants of San Nicolas Island were brought over to the mainland of California. One woman was left behind on the island, and spent the next eighteen years alone. What little we know about the lone woman—how she lived on the island and how she came to leave it—comes from accounts and documents that were recorded at the time of her rescue.

San Nicolas is still a barren and desolate island, sixty-one miles from the coast of California and thirty miles from its nearest neighbor island. Its windswept plains and brush-choked canyons form a wild landscape eight miles long and four miles wide. This oval-shaped island is about fourteen thousand comparatively level acres in size. It is part of the eight Channel Islands, the most famous of which is Santa Catalina Island. The lone woman's tribe called their island Gha-las-hat and had a name for each of the eight islands.

Her lone isolation began on an April morning in 1835. The crew of the sailing ship *Peor es Nada,* which means Better than Nothing, was bringing the Nicoleño Indians on board to take them to the mainland of California as requested by the mission fathers. On board the ship, the woman realized that her child was not in sight. She screamed and signaled that her child was missing. According to some accounts, she raced to the ship's rail and dove overboard into the storming waves to swim back to the shore to rescue her child.

The weather quickly turned worse, and the roughened sea endangered the ship. The crew and Indians aboard braced themselves as the ship pitched and rolled in the building storm. The schooner's position was in danger, and Captain Charles Hubbard decided he could not delay sailing. He gave orders to weigh anchor and sailed away running before the wind, leaving the woman alone on the island.

Captain Hubbard thought he could rescue her on another voyage. But after the *Peor es Nada* delivered the Nicoleño Indians to the mainland, the ship was ordered to Monterey to take a cargo of timber to San Francisco. As the *Peor es Nada* sailed for San Francisco loaded with timber, it capsized and was destroyed. Now there was no ship on the Pacific coast that could successfully negotiate the rough sea to San Nicolas Island. The lone woman's fate was known on the mainland, but soon the people thought she must have perished in the island's harsh climate.

On the island, the woman searched for her child but she was unable to find it. She concluded that the child had been eaten by a wild dog and was so overcome with grief that she lay down and cried for a long time, becoming sick and exhausted.

The lone woman would spend the next eighteen years

alone on the island struggling to take care of all her needs. Her daily routine of life was only varied by her hunger, thirst, and cold. She had no one to talk with or to keep her company.

Her main dwelling was a large cave on the north end of the island. She also had a home made of whales' ribs standing in the sand and covered with brush. The dwellings had been left by her friends and family.

She stored her food in crevices and the fissures of rocks, out of the reach of the island's wild dogs, saving it for those days when she was sick or could not find fresh food. She kept dried meat at each of her camping stations. The tough dried seal meat sanded away her teeth down to her gums. She was skillful at weaving watertight grass baskets to collect fresh, clear water from springs.

She fashioned her dresses from the feathers of cormorants. They were sleeveless, low in the neck, and girded at the waist with a sinew rope. The satiny plumage of feathers pointed downward and extended to her ankles. She skillfully matched the feathers to make one continuous sheen of changeful luster. Her reddish brown hair hung to her shoulders, and she made a rude slate necklace. Although there was no one near to admire or praise her, she wore it and prized it as a great ornament.

She was familiar with the island's birds: ravens, ospreys, eagles, shags, cormorants, snipes, and brown pelicans. Fishing lines made of sinew, and hooks from abalone shells, enabled her to catch and dry seal meat, fish, abalone and other shellfish, sea urchins, and roots. She used implements made and left by her people, including mortars and pestles.

She made fire, essential to her for cooking and warmth, by rapidly rubbing a pointed stick along a groove on a flat stick until a spark was struck. It was a difficult task, and she was

careful not to let her fire go out. She kept her fire going at all times, taking a brand and transporting the fire as she moved to different areas of the island, and she covered her fire with ashes to keep it alive when she was away from camp.

Seventeen years after she was left on the island, in April of 1852, Captain Nidever came by ship to hunt for otters around San Nicolas Island. Large ships were now available for crossing the area's rough waters. As the captain and several members of his crew traveled along the beach they discovered fresh human footprints. Back from the beach, about two miles apart, they found three small circular enclosures made of sage brush. Their thin walls were five feet high and six feet in diameter with a small narrow opening on one side.

Captain Nidever was convinced that someone was on the island. He had heard stories about the abandoned woman and thought it might be her. But a violent storm soon drove the hunters to the shelter of the ship and a calmer harbor. The gale continued for eight days, and finally the captain decided to return to Santa Barbara.

The lone woman watched from her hiding place as they sailed out of sight. She had seen them on the beach but was afraid and hid until they were gone. Now, alone again, she cried in loneliness and regret that she had not made herself known.

On the mainland, Captain Nidever told others of the footprints. Father Gonzalez of the mission offered a reward of two hundred dollars for rescuing the woman.

The following winter Captain Nidever fitted out for another trip to San Nicolas. The captain and crew kept a sharp lookout for the lost woman. They found her large grass basket in the fork of a high bush called malva real. Inside was the cormorant feather dress, bone needles and knives, fishhooks made of abalone shell, and a well-made rope of sinews twisted evenly that measured twenty-five feet in length. The items were placed neatly in the basket.

After they examined each item, they returned them to the basket. Then Captain Nidever suggested, "Scatter the feathers and things in the basket, and if she is alive she will find them." If she were there, he reasoned, the items would be replaced in the basket. They left the items scattered about and returned to their vessel. They became busy hunting otters, and on their fourth day another storm sprang up. After six days the captain decided to set sail to a safer harbor on a nearby island and then headed back home to the mainland again.

The captain made his third trip to the island in the spring of 1853. This time he was determined to search the entire island and either find the woman or know for certain she no longer existed. After anchoring the ship, Captain Nidever, a fisherman named Carl Dittman who was called Charley Brown by the sailors, an Irish cook, and a few of the mission Indians went ashore to pick a site for their camp.

The captain and Charley walked toward the head of the island. Nidever sat down to rest while Charley continued along near the shore. There Charley found and followed footprints until they disappeared in moss. He returned to the captain and told him of his discovery. They decided to search the island the next morning.

After breakfast, all hands, except the cook, went ashore. They discovered the basket, with its contents carefully replaced, in the fork of the malva real where they had discovered it on their previous trip. Charley and the captain returned to the footprints. They knew the slender footprints were too small for a man and that they were recent.

Halfway up a ridge they found a small piece of driftwood. Had she dropped it on her way up the beach with her firewood? Farther up the ridge they found the huts made of whales' ribs.

Charley noticed a small dark shape in the distance and moved toward it. As he came near he saw it was the Indian woman talking to herself. He moved cautiously and approached to within a few yards of her. Two wild dogs growled at his approach, but she calmed them and sent them away with a yell.

She sat cross-legged on the ground, separating blubber from a piece of seal skin that was lying across one knee and held by one hand. In the other hand she grasped a crude knife made of a piece of iron hoop thrust into a rough piece of wood for a handle. Scattered around her were grass baskets and high piles of ashes and bones. A sinew rope stretched between two poles several feet above the ground, and from it were hanging pieces of seal blubber.

After eighteen years of being alone, she seemed pleased to have company. She bowed and smiled, speaking rapidly and moving her arms about. The crew of mission Indians spoke several dialects, but none could understand her. She took roots from her grass sacks and placed them in the coals to roast. When they were cooked she passed them around and made motions for the men to eat.

They helped her pack up all her belongings, filling a basket. She raised it to her back and secured it with straps passing over her shoulders and under her arms. With a load on her back that seemed heavy enough for a mule, she took in one hand a glowing brand and left her home.

During dinner on board the schooner she smacked her lips showing her pleasure. She liked sugar and anything sweet and preferred their bacon and bread to meals of blubber and shell-fish. To replace and preserve her beautiful feather dress, Charley made her a skirt out of ticking and gave her a man's shirt. She wore these as she helped in the daily work by collecting wood and water for herself and the crew. As she worked on her baskets she laughed and talked. She was happy to be with other people again, even though they could not understand each other.

After hunting for a month, the ship and her crew set out for the mainland. On their homeward passage they were met with a gale so violent that at several times Captain Nidever thought they might need to return to the island. The woman signaled that she would stop the wind. Getting on her knees and turning her face in the direction of the storm, she prayed until the wind stopped. With a triumphant smile she pointed to a patch of clear blue sky. Her prayers, she motioned, had been answered.

After the ship's arrival at Santa Barbara, Captain Nidever took the woman into his home, where his wife and children cared for her. The Captain was offered one thousand dollars by a museum wanting to place the woman on exhibit, but he refused all offers. Knowing how lonely her last eighteen years must have been, he wanted to protect her and let her have company with others.

Soon the Nidevers' house was crowded with people who came to see her and the objects she had made and used on the island. She would sing and dance for them wearing her beautiful feather dress. Visitors would give her presents of trinkets and sometimes money, but these were not valued by her. She would take them politely and give them to Captain Nidever's children, happy when the gifts pleased them.

Though she was able to communicate with her visitors through hand and facial gestures, no one could interpret her language to learn more about her solitary life. The Nicoleño Indians who were rescued almost two decades before could not be located. She was disappointed that her family and friends were not found. Perhaps she even missed her outdoor life.

A few weeks after arriving on the mainland she became ill. Maybe it was the change of her diet or the germs from the association with people. Seven weeks to the day after her arrival in Santa Barbara, the lone woman died. They were unable to learn her name, so they named her Juana María. She is buried in the Santa Barbara Mission cemetery, where a plaque commemorating her reads: "Juana María, Indian woman abandoned on San Nicolas Island eighteen years, found and brought to Santa Barbara by Captain George Nidever in 1853."

~~~

A native Californian, **Helen Foster James** *teaches children's literature at San Diego State University, the University of California at San Diego, and National University. She is the author of several resource books, book reviews, and articles.*

Dark Sky

Outside My Coast Boulevard Apartment, La Jolla, California

Marian Haddad

You are the darkest sky
I've seen. You're black,
you're blue, shades and colors
of green. Come down on me
dark sky, bring yourself low,
cover me like a mantilla,
my mother's head cloth.
You are here, dark sky,
above me. Watching.
Covering. Laying yourself
low above my own darkness.
We are both black, sky.
Sky is your name. You see,
I call you by it. Hush.
There are stars beeping
soundless. I cannot hear them,
but I see them. Watch.
Miniscule headlights waning.
On. Off. They would beep
if I could hear them. Listen. Here
a star. There a star. Stars
all around me. My neck is breaking
I've bent it so far back. I am dizzy

with sky. This is my planetarium,
my private ensconcement, my galaxies
shining, my blue, my dark,
my midnight sky. Hush.

Born and raised in the desert town of El Paso, Texas, **Marian Haddad** *thought she would never love anything more than the fire of a desert sunset. Then she moved to La Jolla and discovered the majesty of the Pacific coastline. One night, unable to sleep, she stepped out of her apartment, and "Dark Sky" was born a few feet away from the breaking waves of Wind 'n Sea Beach, under a midnight California sky. A former associate editor for* Poetry International, *she has been published in the* Rio Grande Review, Sin Fronteras/Writers without Borders, *and other publications.*

Coyote and the Acorns

A YUROK STORY

Acorns were once a staple part of the diet of indigenous groups living along the California coast. The fruits of oak trees, acorns are loaded with nutritious calories. But the people who ate them first had to remove the tannins—chemicals that make the acorns bitter and even somewhat toxic. This coyote story from the Yurok people of northern California provides a humorous reflection of how much they valued acorns.

Coyote lived with his grandmother. Once he went away on a visit. They fed him sour acorns. He liked them and asked, "How do you make sour acorns?" So they told him how to prepare them. "You put a little water on them and press them down and about two days later you look at them." But Coyote would not believe that this was how one did it. He said, "I think you do it some other way!" They said, "No, that is the way we do it." But Coyote would not believe them; he kept asking them how sour acorns were really made. After a while they got tired of his always asking about a different way and said to him, "We take the acorns down to the river and put them in a canoe." Then he said, "I knew you did it some other way!" "After you load them into a canoe, you tip it over and drown the acorns." "I knew," Coyote said, "you did it some other way!" "And after a while you walk along the river and you find lots of acorns again."

Coyote believed them and ran to his grandmother to tell her about the sour acorns that he liked. The old woman said, "Yes, you damp them a little and press them hard. That is how they get sour." But Coyote said, "No, I know a different way to sour them. You take the acorns to the river and put them in a canoe and drown them." My! That old woman was angry. Coyote took all those acorns down to the river. He was going

to put them into a canoe. The old woman hid some of the acorns.

Coyote drowned his acorns. After he had drowned them he went along the river, thinking that he would find them, but he never found them. He went to his grandmother afterwards and told her about it. The old woman was angry. Coyote nearly starved. Whenever he went somewhere the old woman pounded acorns and soaked them. She had acorns ready now, but she would not feed him.

Coyote made a fire in the sweat-house. The old woman thought, "He's in the sweat-house, I'm going to cook those acorns." And she cooked the acorns. Coyote smelled them from the sweat-house. He ran out. The old woman heard someone coming as the acorns were boiling. She threw blankets on top of the basket and sat down on it. She was not going to let him eat. Coyote came in. "What are you cooking, grandma?" "Nothing." "I smell acorns. Yes, you have lots of acorns!" He stood around. "I hear something boiling." "No," said the old woman, "my stomach is growling." "No," he said, "I hear something boiling underneath you." "I had a little accident," she said this time. But Coyote seized her and lifted her up. He found the acorns. He ate them, for he was almost starved.

⌣⌢

This story is adapted from a story narrated by a Yurok woman named Mrs. Haydom in the summer of 1927.

Wild Lives

Swimming Lessons

Harbor Seals, Point Reyes National Seashore

JEFFREY HARRISON

They could be driftwood from this far above,
strewn on that crescent of beach at the cliff's base,
bleached gray. Except that now and then they move:
a pup and mother bounce until they reach
the water, and flop in. Then we see other
swerving forms—each pup clinging to its mother
or swimming alongside, or playing chase,
until a breaker rolls them up the beach.

We watch and watch, but it's never long enough.
And our binoculars aren't strong enough:
we want to be *among* them in the surf,
swimming through kelp—that would be happiness.
No matter when it comes, our leaving is
an interruption, like the cliff between us.

Jeffrey Harrison *is the author of three collections of poetry,* The Singing Underneath *(1988, a National Poetry Series selection),* Signs of Arrival *(1996), and* Feeding the Fire *(Sarabande Books, 2001). He currently lives in Massachusetts with his wife, son, and daughter.*

Seacoast Secret

Nancy Dawson

Many mammal species that inhabited the California Coast for thousands of years were hunted to near extinction by the mid- to late-nineteenth century. One of the great triumphs of conservation is that some of those animals have made a comeback. This story, based on actual events, describes one such return.

We halted our horses at the edge of the sandstone cliffs and looked out at the Pacific Ocean. A huge wave slammed into black rocks and shot a spray of white foam skyward. The wave continued coming in until it shattered against the rocks beneath the cliffs. The churning foam scampered back out and was lost in the collision with the next wave crashing shoreward.

I raised my binoculars. "Tim, look! There's something swimming out by the rocks. It just dove under. Now I can't find it."

"Probably a sea lion. Come on, Kate, let's go. I want to get in some fishing before the sun sets."

I didn't want to leave the ocean, but Tim was my older brother, and today he was the boss. It was June 1935; he was sixteen and I was fourteen. I was feeling quite grown-up, as this was the first time our parents had agreed to let us ride over to the ocean from our cattle ranch and camp out overnight without them.

We turned inland and rode a mile north before stopping on the banks of Bixby Creek to set up camp. Tim went upstream to fish. My passions pulled me the other way, back to the ocean and its unending watery horizon.

As I rode Star Blazer along the creek toward the ocean, my mind filled with the creatures of the sea. In my imagination, stingrays, sharks, and octopuses battled with slimy sea monsters and mermaids.

My imagination. Dad thought it was a problem, past time for me to put my fantasies and sketchpad aside and focus on the real world. Momma wanted me to work harder on my studies and spend more time with her in the kitchen, baking bread and canning vegetables. Tim liked my fanciful drawings well enough, but he pestered me to make more of Star Blazer, of the pigs and the barn. Me, I liked to draw what is not there, the unseen.

The whoosh and whirrr of the waves and the kur-kree! of the seagulls broke into my thoughts. Bixby Creek cut a path through the sand and emptied into the ocean. I slowed Star Blazer to a walk and breathed in the salty air and bitter odor of seaweed marooned by high tide and now rotting under the sun.

I stared hard at the kelp beds in a bay near shore. Something long and brown floated there. Driftwood maybe, or something alive. I raised my binoculars and scanned until I had the kelp bed in view.

Then I saw it: A brown furry creature floating on its back. Its head was round with chubby cheeks and tiny dark eyes. It had a large brown nose surrounded by white hair and whiskers.

Hands! The creature had furry hands with fingerlike claws. I sucked in a deep breath. Had I really seen hands?

Now the hands lay hidden under the water as the creature swam on its back, propelled by strokes from hind flippers. The creature rolled over and dove beneath the waves.

I panned my binoculars back across the kelp bed. There! Three more of the creatures back-floating, each wrapped in a kelp frond with only its head protruding. Why? Were they cold? Trapped by the huge seaweed? Dead, and this was their burial tomb? I imagined the wrapping rite, kelp spun round and round by tiny hands.

But as I watched, two of the creatures rolled over until they were free of the kelp. They swam and chased after each other, nipping and nudging, just like children playing tag. Finally, they dove out of sight.

Star Blazer whinnied and I noticed the sun was setting. Time to go.

When I got back to our campsite, I jumped down and tied Star Blazer's reins to the twisted limb of a cypress tree.

"Tim! I saw the most amazing sea creatures! They were round and brown and furry and looked like bear cubs floating on their backs."

"Ummm . . . how about cleaning these fish while I build a fire?" He handed me his pocketknife and I slit open a steelhead trout.

"They chased each other and dove under the waves and . . ."

"Probably sea lions," he said. "Maybe they were mating."

"No, they weren't sea lions!"

"Kate, bear cubs floating in the ocean? Sounds like your imagination played tricks on your eyes in the fading light."

"No, these are real! I'll show them to you tomorrow before we ride home."

But the next morning our campsite was wrapped in a dense layer of fog so thick that the horses looked like ghosts though they were only twenty feet away. No point in trying to go to the ocean. The damp fog made my hair frizzy and wild. I tied it up with a scarf and managed to get a fire going for breakfast. Then we packed up camp, saddled our horses, and rode slowly into the fog, inland toward our cattle ranch.

Tim and I rode close together, singing songs and telling jokes to keep from getting separated. After an hour the fog thinned. Near the top of a hill, we broke through to sunshine. I turned in my saddle and looked back west. Fog still blanketed the hills and ravines. We rode east, into the warmth.

We arrived home in time for Tim to milk the cow and me to set the table for supper. While we ate, I told my parents about the sea creatures.

"Probably sea lions," said Dad, siding with Tim.

"No, they weren't! They were rounder and furry and had the cutest little hands," I said.

"You can look for them in the encyclopedia," said Momma. That's Momma, always making something into a school lesson, even in the summer.

"Or you can look for them in your fairy tale books," said Tim with a smirk. I shot him a dark look and got even by cutting him a particularly small piece of strawberry-rhubarb pie.

After washing the dishes, I opened the glass doors of the bookcase and pulled out volume five of *Compton's Pictured Encyclopedia.* I looked up "marine life." No listing.

Next I tried "ocean." Pictures of snails and corals and

seaweeds. Drawings of eels and jellyfish. But no furry bears floating on their backs.

I looked up "sea" and found "sea anemones," with a lovely drawing of the straggly, flowerlike animals. I got out my sketchpad and began to draw them, attached to rocks and waving their long tentacles in the ocean currents. Then it was bedtime.

The next morning as Momma and I kneaded dough and shaped it into bread loaves, I told her about my futile search through the encyclopedia.

"Well," she said, "you could write a letter to the biologists up at Stanford University. Surely they would know."

While the loaves rose, I wrote the letter. I drew a picture of the sea creatures at the bottom. Three days later, a neighbor stopped by on his way to Carmel and took my letter in to the post office.

My summer days after that were filled with weeding the garden, baking bread, washing mounds of dishes, and, when I had time, riding Star Blazer around the ranch or drawing in my sketchpad. I was not allowed to ride the fifteen miles over to the ocean by myself, and Tim and my parents were too busy to go with me.

A month passed before Dad had time to drive into Carmel to buy supplies and pick up our mail. He had a letter for me when he returned!

Dear Miss Kelly,

Thank you for your letter, which was forwarded to me by the Department of Biological Sciences at Stanford University. I am going to be in your area doing some research and will stop by your ranch August 20th.

Until then, it is of the utmost importance that you do not talk to anyone about what you saw. I will tell you all about it when I come to visit.

Sincerely,
Dr. Philip Backus
Hopkins Marine Station
Pacific Grove, California

"A matter of utmost importance! I'm going to be famous!" I read the letter to my family and danced around the kitchen.

The wait for Dr. Backus was agonizing. Momma said the time would go faster if I kept busy, her excuse for giving me more chores.

Dr. Backus finally drove up just before supper on the 20th. After brief introductions, he turned to me.

"Your drawing is quite good," he said. "Here, take a look at these pictures." He handed me a thick book, opened to a spread of illustrations.

"Yes! That's it!" I shouted, pointing.

"California sea otters," he said.

"Sea otters? But they're extinct," said Momma.

"Not quite. They were heavily hunted, but a few survived," Dr. Backus replied. "I've been observing the raft of otters over by Bixby Creek for the last two days. I counted twenty-four adults, but no pups."

"If they're not extinct, how come nobody around here knows about them?" asked Tim.

"The few scientists who know about the existence of sea otters are keeping quiet. Sea otters are now protected by law, but we're afraid that poachers would hunt them if the word gets out," Dr. Backus said. "That's why it's so important that you tell no one."

After supper, we heard about how sea otters were relentlessly hunted for their thick fur, which was made into luxurious coats and hats.

"Why do they wrap up in kelp?" I asked.

"So they don't drift away while they're sleeping. The kelp fronds are attached to the ocean floor," explained Dr. Backus.

Before leaving the next morning, Dr. Backus asked us to send him information about any otter sightings: the number, date, location, and their behavior. He had each one of us solemnly swear that we would not reveal the sea otter secret.

The next Saturday, Dad left the hired hands in charge of the ranch. My family saddled horses and rode over to the ocean to look for sea otters. We took turns with the binoculars and rode in pairs up and down the beach, our eyes always scanning the ocean. We saw a few sea lions sunbathing on the rocks, seagulls skimming just above the waves, black cormorants flying low and diving for fish, but no sea otters.

Sunday morning, we made one more ride down the beach.

"There!" shouted Tim, pointing at a sea otter swimming on its back. I looked through the binoculars.

"A baby! There's a baby riding on the otter's stomach!" I passed the binoculars to Momma.

"Mother and child," she whispered.

We watched until they swam out of sight.

"Time to go," said Dad reluctantly. "Thank you, Kate, for bringing us the sea otter secret."

"Hey, Kate, you should draw a new picture and send it to Dr. Backus," said Tim. "He will want to know about the baby."

"Right," said Dad, "Good thing we have an artist in the family."

Note: California sea otters were hunted to near extinction by the mid-1800s. The few twentieth-century scientists who knew about isolated populations of sea otters remained silent, fearing that the last survivors would also be hunted. The secret held until 1938 when a rancher announced that he had spotted otters near Bixby Creek, thirteen miles south of Carmel. Coastal Highway 1 from Monterey to San Simeon had just opened, and the sea otters became a major sightseeing attraction. Since then, the number of California sea otters has slowly increased to between 2,000 and 2,400 during the 1990s. "Seacoast Secret" is fiction, based on these historical facts.

Nancy Dawson *loves the open landscapes and sweeping skies of the West. She lives and writes in Boulder, Colorado.*

Bougainvillea in L.A.

Stefi Weisburd

Even on the gray walls
of freeways, pocked
with gang scribbles and scrawls
you unfurl yourself regally
like a Flamenco dancer's
flamingo-colored shawl.
Rice paper blossoms
bright as castanets
beat fiery orange,
vibrant vermilion, bronze.
Bougainvillea, you spill
over the concrete sea
as if you were the sun's graffiti.

Stefi Weisburd *grew up in California. She was an editor at* Science News *magazine, and her stories have appeared in the* Los Angeles Times, Business Week, Health, Parenting, *and other magazines. Her children's poems have or will appear in* Cricket, Ladybug, Highlights, *and* Hopscotch.

Invocation

JANE HIRSHFIELD

This August night, raccoons,
come to the back door
burnished all summer by salty,
human touch: enter secretly & eat.

Listen, little mask-faced ones,
unstealthy bandits whose tails
are barred with dusk:
listen, gliding green-eyed ones:
I concede you gladly
all this much-handled stuff,
garbage, grain,
the cropped food and cropped heart—
may you gnaw in contentment
through the sleep-hours
on everything left out.

May you find the house
hospitable,
well-used,
stocked with sufficient goods.
I'll settle with your leavings,

as you have settled for mine,
before startling back into darkness
that marks each of us so differently.

Jane Hirshfield *is the author of four books of poetry and a collection of essays. She has lived in northern California for more than twenty-five years.*

Left Sink

Ellery Akers

Most of the Pacific tree frogs that live along the California coast spend the dry season curled up beneath the soil in a state of semihibernation. But a few individuals opt for a more peculiar choice of summer habitat.

The first time I saw Left Sink I was brushing my teeth and almost spit on him. I wasn't expecting to find a frog in a Park Service bathroom, but there he was, hopping out of the drain and squatting on the porcelain as casually as if he were sitting beside a pond.

He was a small green tree frog, no bigger than a penny, and his round, salmon-colored toes stuck out like tiny soupspoons. For a few minutes I stared into his gold eyes, each pupil floating in the middle like a dark seed.

I was so close I could see his throat pulse, but I was probably too close, for he looked at me fearfully and leaped onto the silver "C" of the cold-water faucet.

Then he must have thought better of it, for he jumped down again, and sat, hunched over, by the soap. He kept making nervous little hops toward the safety of the drain, but my looming face was obviously in the way, so I ducked below the basin for a moment, and when I looked again he was descending into the hole, head first.

Feeling I'd disturbed his evening hunt, I decided to make amends. I grubbed around the floor for a dead moth, found one (though it was a little dried up), and offered it to the hole. The wing slanted into the drain, but nothing happened. I thought perhaps he'd hopped back down into the pipe. Trying to find something a little more appealing, I picked around the windowsills until I discovered a really decent-looking moth, pushed it up to the drain, and waited. After a few minutes, I got discouraged and walked away. When I turned back to sneak one last look, both moths had vanished.

The next day was so hot I forgot Left Sink completely. It is always hot in the California chaparral in September, especially in the Galiban Mountains. I spent the afternoon in the shade, lying on the cool pebbles of a dry wash and looking over my field notes. I had been camping for weeks, studying birds, and by now I had gotten used to the feeling of expectation in the landscape.

Everything seemed to be waiting for rain. The streambeds were dry, the fields were dry, and when the buckeye leaves hissed in the wind they sounded like rattlesnakes. Ravens flew overhead, croaking, their wings flapping loudly in the air. The rocks baked. Once in a while a few thirsty finches fluttered up to a seep in a cliff and sipped from a damp clump of algae.

I leaned against the cool flank of a boulder and fanned myself with my hat. From far away I could hear the staccato drill of a Nuttall's woodpecker. All the animals had some way of coping with the heat. The wrentits could last for several weeks without drinking. The deer found beds of shade and waited patiently until evening. Even the trees adapted. I knew that somewhere beneath my boots, one hundred feet down, the root of a digger pine was twisting along a crevice in the bedrock, reaching far below the surface to tap into the water table.

And the Pacific tree frogs—the normal ones—were sleeping away the summer and fall, huddled in some moist spot in the ground in a kind of hot-weather hibernation.

That night, when I went back to the bathroom, I discovered Left Sink had neighbors. Just before I turned on the water in the right-hand basin I noticed a second frog, and when I stepped back to look at both of them in their respective sinks, I started to laugh: They reminded me of a couple of sober, philosophical old monks peering out of their cells.

Overhead was a third frog, puffy and well-fed, squatting on top of the fluorescent lights, surrounded by tattered moths. I decided to call him the Light Buddha.

In the world of the bathroom, the light shelf was a delicatessen of the highest order, and the Light Buddha sat there night after glorious night, lazily snapping up moths as they fluttered past. The other two frogs seemed content to stake out the sinks, which weren't quite as dependable a food source, though they weren't bad. Almost every night I found a damp moth thrashing around in one of the basins, one little flopping death after another.

Right Sink was extremely shy, and spent most of his time crouched far back in the pipe. Usually I saw his gold eyes shining in the darkness, but that was all. Left Sink was more of an adventurer and explored the whole bathroom, darting behind the mirror, splatting onto the porcelain, hopping onto the windowsills, leaping onto the toilet, and climbing the slippery painted walls toe pad by toe pad.

From time to time I was tempted to pick him up as he was

climbing. But I didn't think it would be fair; I knew this geo-metrical universe, and he didn't. Besides, there was no place for him to hide on those smooth, painted bricks. Even though tree frogs can change color in ten minutes, there was nothing in Left Sink's repertoire that could possibly match white paint; the best he could do was a sickly pink.

I could always tell if he had just emerged from the drain be-cause he would still be a murky gray-green. As the evening wore on he got paler and paler. Once I couldn't find him for half an hour. Finally I caught sight of him over my head. Plopped on a narrow ledge, he looked like a pale pebble in all that metal and paint. I climbed onto the toilet for a better look. To my horror he began hopping along the ledge, which was no wider than half an inch. It was a ten-foot fall to the floor—for a frog that small, an abyss. He bounded past me, his grainy throat quiver-ing. He headed toward a swarm of moths and flies that circled the fluorescent lights. A fly drifted down from the glare; Left Sink, his pink mouth flashing, snapped it up.

I was never quite sure just how skittish he really was. Sometimes he tolerated my watching him, sometimes he didn't. I got in the habit of sidling up to the plumbing, bent over so as not to be seen, and I must have looked pretty pecu-liar. One night a woman came into the bathroom and caught me hunched over like Quasimodo, staring intently at the drains, my hands full of dead moths.

"Left Sink! Right Sink!" I was saying. "Got a little treat for you guys!"

The woman bolted out the door.

I checked on the frogs every morning and evening. Sometimes when I saw Left Sink skidding down a length of plastic, unable to hold on in spite of his adhesive toe pads, I

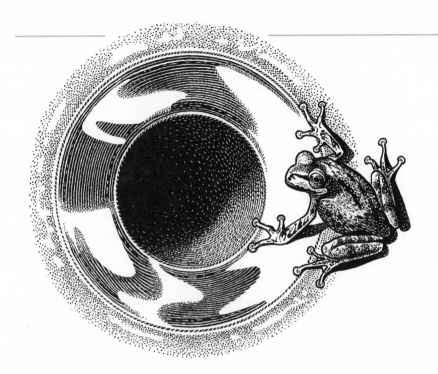

worried. I couldn't help thinking there was something unnat-
ural about a frog in a bathroom.

Of course, I knew there were a few oddballs that had managed to live with us in our artificial world, but they were
mostly insects. One year in school I had learned about the
larvae of petroleum flies: They live in the gunk of oil fields, so
numerous at times that, according to my textbook, they im-
parted "a shimmering effect to the surface of the oil." Their
world was oil; if you deprived them of it, took them out and
cleaned them off, they'd curl up and die in less than a day.

In that same class I'd learned that furniture beetles live in
our table legs, and occasionally in wooden spoons; drugstore
beetles float happily in bottles of belladonna, mating, pupat-
ing, dying. We have cheese mites in our cheese, and flour mites
in our flour.

But no one mentioned anything about frogs.

Actually, considering the drought, Left Sink had a pretty good setup. It was already October and still no rain. Once in a while a few drops would plop into the dirt and gravel, and I would catch a whiff of wet dust, soaked cheat grass, and buckwheat. But that was all.

All the other frogs were holed up in the dirt, huddled in a moist crack or an abandoned gopher hole, waiting for the first rains of winter to wake them up. There were probably a few hiding in the field next to Left Sink's bathroom, their eyelids closed, their toes pulled under them to conserve moisture, unmoving, barely breathing, their heartbeats almost completely stilled. If I dug them up they would look like small stones.

One night just before I was about to leave the campground, I had a nightmare. It was a dream I had had many times, a dream of a city so polluted the air rose in black plumes above the granite and cement. I was at the entrance of a tunnel. Inside I could hear a whoosh of air. Millions of butterflies were flashing in the dark, thousands of ducks, eagles, sparrows, their wings making a vast rustling as they flew off and vanished.

I heard a low shuffling. After a while I realized it was the sound of feet: the slow trudge of bears, the pad of badgers, the pattering of foxes, the rasp of a hundred million beetles, rabbits, ants, mice. I looked around, panicked, to see if any animals were left. There were still cockroaches scuttling over the windowsills. There were pigeons, flies, starlings. I named them over and over in a kind of chant: the adaptable, the drab, the ones who could live with us, who had always lived with us.

A fox coughed close to my camp and woke me up. I unzipped the tent and looked out at the stars: Rigel, Algol, clear, cold, and changeless. A golden-crowned sparrow chirped from a nearby branch, then sputtered off into silence. For a while I tried to stay awake, but soon drifted off.

The next morning huge bluish clouds rolled across the sky. A couple of ravens sailed past the cliff in front of me. One of them jackknifed its wings, plummeted straight down, and then, at the last minute, unfolded them and flapped away. It was still early, but when I reached the bathroom it had already been cleaned. It reeked of ammonia, and a mop and bucket leaned against the door.

I rinsed off my face, brushed my hair, and looked sleepily into the drains. As usual, Right Sink was huddled far back into the dark pipe; he retreated still farther when I bent over.

Left Sink, however, was gone. I wondered if he had slipped behind the mirror, or had come up in the world and was squatting with the Light Buddha. The shelf was empty. I looked on the windowsill—not there either.

It was not until I opened the door to the toilet that I found him. There, in the center of the ammonia-filled bowl, his green bloated body turning gray, was Left Sink, splayed out in the milky liquid, dead. Floating in front of him was a dead damselfly. I suppose he must have jumped in after his prey, convinced he was at the edge of a strange-looking pond, his toe pads gripping the cold, perfectly smooth surface of the porcelain.

His skin looked curdled, and it occurred to me that he might have been there all morning, waiting to die. Then I remembered that frogs breathe through their skin; it must have been a hard, stinging death, but a quick one.

I flushed him down, wishing I could think of something to say as he made his way through the pipes and rolled out to the septic tank, some acknowledgment of the link between my kind and his, but I couldn't think of anything except that I would miss him, which was true.

When I opened the door a couple of nervous towhees blundered into the bushes. It was beginning to rain.

Ellery Akers *is a writer, artist, and naturalist living in Marin County, California. She has won five national awards for poetry, and her book of poems,* Knocking on Earth, *was published by Wesleyan University Press. Her nature essays have appeared in* Sierra *and* Pacific Discovery.

Entomológica

Roberto Castillo Udiarte

Las arañas se han apoderado
de cada rincón de casa.
No tienen prisa,
no se mueven de su lugar,
el tiempo es de ellas.
Patas arriba, tejen la llegada
del insecto imprudente.
El privilegio de las arañas
es saber esperar.

Entomological

The spiders have taken over
each corner of the house.
They're not in a hurry,
they don't move from their places,
time is theirs.
Upside down, they weave the arrival
of an imprudent insect.
The privilege of the spiders
is knowing how to wait.

A poet from northwestern Mexico, **Roberto Castillo Udiarte** *frequently writes about social issues.*

The Dolphins

Near the Channel Islands, California

DAVID MEUEL

I blinked,
and there they were,
dozens and scores of them
inviting us
to share a dance
upon a floor
of bright, slapping sea.
Following their lead,
our boat stepped right,
then left, then right again.
Guiding us stride for stride,
they sprang and darted and dove
in chorus lines
of two and three and four.
And together,
we twirled the sea
around the sun.

David Meuel *is the author of* Islands in the Sky, *which won first place in the poetry category in the 1997 National Self-Published Books Awards sponsored by* Writer's Digest Magazine. *A lifetime resident of the San Francisco Bay Area, David works as an executive speechwriter and lives with his wife and son in Palo Alto, California.*

A-Birding on a Bronco

FLORENCE A. MERRIAM

*Florence Merriam spent the spring of 1894 studying birds on her uncle's
ranch in northern San Diego County. Her adventures and observations
became the subject of her book,* A-Birding on a Bronco, *from which
this piece is drawn.*

"Climb the mountain back of the house and you can see the
Pacific," the ranchman told me with a gleam in his eye; and
later, when I had done that, from the top of a peak at the foot
of the valley he pointed out the distant blue mountains of
Mexico. Then he gave me his daughter's saddle horse to use as
long as I was his guest, that I might explore the valley and
study its birds to the best advantage. Before coming to
California, I had known only the birds of New York and
Massachusetts, and so was filled with eager enthusiasm at the
thought of spending the migration and nesting season in a
new bird world.

I had no gun, but was armed with opera-glass and note-
book, and had Ridgway's Manual to turn to in all my perplex-
ities. Every morning, right after breakfast, my horse was
brought to the door and I set out to make the rounds of the
valley. I rode till dinner time, getting acquainted with the migrants as they came from the south, and calling at the more

distant nests on the way. After dinner I would take my camp-stool and stroll through the oaks at the head of the valley, for a quiet study of the nearer nests. Then once more my horse would be brought up for me to take a run before sunset; and at night I would identify my new birds and write up the notes of the day. What more could observer crave? The world was mine. I never spent a happier spring. The freedom and novelty of ranch life and the exhilaration of days spent in the saddle gave added zest to the delights of a new fauna. In my small valley circuit of a mile and a half, I made the acquaintance of about seventy-five birds, and without resort to the gun was able to name fifty-six of them.

My saddle horse, a white bronco who went by the musical name of Canello, . . . was warranted to stand still before a flock of birds so long as there was grass to eat. He was to be relied on as a horse of ripe experience and mature judgment in matters of local danger. No power of bit or spur could induce him to set foot upon a piece of 'boggy land,' and to give me confidence one of the ranchman's sons said, "Wherever I've killed a rattlesnake from him he'll shy for years;" and went on to cite localities where a sudden, violent lurch had nearly sent him over Canello's head! What greater recommendation could I wish? . . .

Canello and I soon became the best of friends. I found in him a valuable second—for, as I had anticipated, the birds were used to grazing horses, and were much less suspicious of an equestrian than a foot passenger—and he found in me a movable stake, constantly leading him to new grazing ground; for when there was a nest to watch I simply hung the bridle over the pommel and let him eat, so getting free hands for opera-glass and note-book. To be sure, there were slight causes of difference between us. He liked to watch birds in the high alfalfa under the sycamores, but when it came to standing still where the hot sun beat down through the brush and there was nothing to eat, his interest in ornithology flagged perceptibly. Then he sometimes carried the role of grazing horse too far, marching off to a fresh clump of grass out of sight of my nest at the most interesting moment; or when I was intently gazing through my glass at a rare bird, he would sometimes give a sudden kick at a horsefly, bobbing the glass out of range just as I was making out the character of the wing-bars.

From the ranch-house, encircled by live-oaks, the valley widened out, and was covered with orchards and vineyards, enclosed by the low brush-grown ridges of the Coast Mountains. It was a veritable paradise for the indolent field student. With so much insect-producing verdure, birds were everywhere at all times. There were no long hours to sit waiting on a camp-stool, and only here and there a treetop to 'sky' the wandering birds. The only difficulty was to choose your intimates.

Canello and I had our regular beat, down past the blooming quince and apricot orchard, along the brush-covered side of the valley where the migrants flocked, around the circle through a great vineyard in the middle of the valley, past a pond where the feathered settlers gathered to bathe, and so back home to the oaks again.

I liked to start out in the freshness of the morning, when the fog was breaking up into buff clouds over the mountains and drawing off in veils over the peaks. The brush we passed through was full of glistening spiders' webs, and in the open the grass was overlaid with disks of cobweb, flashing rainbow colors in the sun.

As we loped gayly along down the curving road, a startled quail would call out, "Who-are-you'-ah? Who-are-you'-ah?" and another would cry "quit" in sharp warning tones; while a pair would scud across the road like little hens, ahead of the horse; or perhaps a covey would start up and whirr over the hillside. The sound of Canello's flying hoofs would often rouse a long-eared jack-rabbit, who with long leaps would go bounding over the flowers, to disappear in the brush.

The narrow road wound through the dense bushy under-growth known as "chaparral," and as Canello galloped round the sharp curves I had to bend low under the sweeping branches, keeping alert for birds and animals. . . .

This corner of the valley was the mouth of Twin Oaks Canyon, and was a forest of brush, alive with birds, and visited only by the children whose small schoolhouse stood beside the giant twin oak from which the valley post-office was named. Flocks of migrating warblers were always to be found here; flycatchers shot out at passing insects; chewinks scratched among the dead leaves and flew up to sing on the branches; insistent vireos cried *tu-whip' tu-whip' tu-whip' tu-wee'-ah*, coming out in sight for a moment only to go hunting back into the impenetrable chaparral; lazuli buntings sang their musical round; blue jays—blue squawkers, as they are here called—went screaming harshly through the thicket; and the clear ringing voice of the wren-tit ran down the scale, now in the brush, now echoing from the boulder-strewn hills above. But the king of the chaparral was the great brown thrasher. His loud rollicking song and careless independent ways, so suggestive of his cousin, the mockingbird, made him always a marked figure.

There was one dense corner of the thicket where a thrasher lived, and I used to urge Canello through the tangle almost every morning for the pleasure of sharing his good spirits. He was not hard to find, big brown bird that he was, standing on the top of a bush as he shouted out boisterously, *kick'-it-now, kick'-it-now, shut'-up shut'-up, dor'-a-thy dor'-a-thy;* or, calling a halt in his mad rhapsody, slowly drawled out, *whoa'-now, whoa'-now.* After listening to such a tirade as this, it was pleasant to come to an opening in the brush and find a band of gentle yellow-birds leaning over the blossoms of the white forget-me-nots.

There were a great many hummingbirds in the chaparral, and at a certain point on the road I was several times attacked by one of the pugnacious little warriors. I suppose we were treading too near his nest, though I was not keen-eyed enough to find it. From high in the air, he would come with a whirr, swooping down so close over our heads that Canello started uneasily and wanted to get out of the way. Down over our heads, and then high up in the air, he would swing back and forth in an arc. One day he must have shot at us half a dozen times, and another day, over a spot in the brush near us,— probably where the nest was,—he did the same thing a dozen times in quick succession.

In the midst of the brush corner were a number of pretty round oaks, in one of which the warblers gathered. My favorite tree was in blossom and alive with buzzing insects, which may have accounted for the presence of the warblers. While I sat in the saddle watching the dainty birds decked out in black and gold, Canello rested his nose in the cleft of the tree, quite unmindful of the busy warblers that flitted about the branches, darting up for insects or chasing down by his nose after falling millers. . . .

On our morning round, Canello and I attended strictly to business,—he to grazing, I to observing; but on our afternoon rides I, at least, felt that we might pay a little more heed to the beauties of the valley and the joys of horsebacking. Sometimes we would be overtaken by the night fog. One moment the mustard would be all aglow with sunshine; at the next, a sullen bank of gray fog would have risen over the mountain, obscuring the sun which had warmed us and lighted the mustard; and in a few moments it would be so cold and damp that I would urge Canello into a lope to warm our blood as we hurried home.

Florence A. Merriam was born in 1863 into a family of naturalists, and soon became an exuberant ornithologist. While attending Smith College, she organized a club to protest the killing of birds for fashion, which subsequently became the first official chapter of the Audubon Society. Merriam, who later wrote under her married name of Florence Merriam Bailey, published many articles and books about birds, including Birds through an Opera Glass, A-Birding on a Bronco, and Birds of New Mexico.

The Poppy

DAN HARDER

Perhaps its
             Fragile
strength lies
             in its petals
     exclusively
             as if each were
  in being so perfectly
             the wing of a monochrome
          suited
                moth . . . suited
to a place of brief floods
             in an iridescent
      and overwhelming
                silk-like orange
        sun.

Dan Harder *considers writing to be a form of directed daydreaming. He's been lucky enough to have a number of his "daydreams" published, including two children's books, two books of essays, two books of poetry, and a number of featured articles in various newspapers and magazines. As for the form of "The Poppy," take it apart and it should make sense; put it together and it should still make sense but it should also make visual music.*

Ode to a Plain Old Pond Frog

WILLIAM PITT ROOT

Your singing sounds
like burping
from the back row
in a class of reeds and mud

Your skin wrinkles
greenly over your bones
like spinach stretching
over a baseball

Legs like a kangaroo's
spring you to the moon
where it ripples
in the center of the pond

Here is what your lovesongs
sound like:
>   *you are ugly*
>   *i love you*
>   *you are ugly*
>   *i love you*

William Pitt Root's *first five books are gathered in his most recent book,* Trace Elements from a Recurring Kingdom *(1994). He lives in Tucson, where he is poet laureate, and teaches at Hunter College in Manhattan, commuting weekly.*

There Oughter Be an Otter!

Olga Cossi

Many people have had the opportunity to see sea otters up close at aquariums. But there is nothing quite like the sight of a sea otter in the wild, floating on its back, a bundle of life on the wide blue water.

Walking is one of the best ways to see what you can see, especially when you live near the ocean. On our very first walk after moving to Santa Cruz, California, we spotted a sea otter in the channel leading in and out of the boat harbor. From then on, these mammals have been a part of our life. "There oughter be an otter!" we joke, and off we go to the sea to see what we can see.

If you have ever watched an otter you know how easily that can become a habit. They float on their backs eating whatever they found on their last dive. Here in the harbor, it is usually a clam or mussel. Up comes the otter with a rock in one paw and a shell in the other. Then he proceeds to use the rock to crack the shell, all the while floating lazily on his back. Boats slip by, all kinds of them, yachts, skiffs, sailboats, catamarans, canoes, and kayaks. The otter goes right on doing what he "oughter" do, which is enjoy the meal waiting for him on his chest.

It is the way they handle their food that keeps us walking down to the harbor day after day. Their forepaws are rather

small, yet they work very quickly to get at the meat. They have to work quickly because there is always a seagull treading water nearby waiting to snatch the tidbit and fly off.

We didn't think that a bird as big as a seagull could actually steal from those busy paws until we saw it happen. We were watching the shell-cracking process when suddenly one of the gulls swooped down, and before the otter could flip over, the bird was flying off with his stolen meal. Never mind. The otter dove again and soon came up with another shell, and another rock.

There is always an otter in among the boats anchored in the harbor, so one day we asked a fisherman if it was the same otter we were seeing or if there were several. He told us that there is a large group, or raft, of these marine mammals here in Santa Cruz, but that there is also a resident otter, one that rarely leaves the channel to swim out to sea. Otters, he told us, do not migrate. They stay in the same coastal area where they were born. They mate and bear their young nearby year after year.

He told us that once when the otter population got to be too much for the local fishermen, someone persuaded the authorities to trap the sea mammals and relocate them hundreds of miles away. This was done. Immediately the entire raft of otters started swimming back. Most of them made it, but many lost their lives trying to get home. When will we humans ever learn?

One reason otters do not migrate is because of their special fur. It is so dense it protects them from extreme cold temperatures that drive other species of sea mammals to find warmer waters. Not only is the fur dense, measuring an average of five hundred thousand hairs per square inch, but there is a layer of air trapped between the skin and the pelt that provides excellent insulation. We often get close enough to our resident harbor otter to admire his luxurious fur. That and his sleek torpedo shape and flippers make him a beautiful swimmer to watch.

Otters teach us many things. Perhaps the nicest lesson they have to teach is to lie back and enjoy whatever you are doing at the moment. You don't always have to be swimming upstream against the current. Stay put once in a while. Just float when you have a chance. Explore what you have at hand. And don't let a noisy audience disturb you.

There "oughter" be an otter in everyone's life.

Olga Cossi *has published several books for young readers, including* Harp Seals, *which was judged as "most outstanding children's science trade book" by the Children's Book Council and the National Science Teachers Association; and* The Magic Box *and* Water Wars, *which were selected by the New York Public Library for their "Books for the Teenage" list.*

Appendixes

✣

Ecology of the
California Coast

What Is an Ecoregion?

The *Stories from Where We Live* series celebrates the literature of North America's diverse ecoregions. Ecoregions are large geographic areas that share similar climate, soils, and plant and animal communities. Thinking ecoregionally helps us understand how neighboring cities and states are connected, and makes it easier to coordinate the use and protection of shared rivers, forests, watersheds, mountain ranges, and other natural areas. We believe that ecoregions also provide an illuminating way to organize and compare place-based literature.

While many institutions have mapped the world's ecoregions, no existing delineation of ecoregions (or similar unit, such as *provinces* or *bioregions*) proved perfectly suited to a literary series. We created our own set of ecoregions based largely on existing scientific designations, with an added consideration for regional differences in human culture.

NORTHWEST

PACIFIC

COAST

CALIFORNIA

COAST

HAWAIIAN

ISLANDS

THE

BOREAL

ROCKY MOUNTAINS

GREAT

NORTH

WESTERN

DESERTS

AND

PLATEAUS

ARCTIC

FOREST

GREAT LAKES

AMERICAN

PRAIRIE

NORTHEAST WOODLANDS

NORTH

ATLANTIC

COAST

APPALACHIAN HIGHLANDS

SOUTH
ATLANTIC
COAST
AND
PIEDMONT

SOUTHERN
HILL
COUNTRY

GULF COAST

Defining the California Coast

If you ask coastal Californians what they like best about their home, most of them will probably mention the weather. Warm summers, mild winters, and plenty of bright sunshine have long drawn people to communities along the California Coast. This Mediterranean climate is one of the key features that defines the California Coast ecoregion.

Mediterranean conditions exist in only five parts of the world: southwestern Australia, the coast of South Africa, the west coast of Chile, the Mediterranean areas of Europe, and the coast of California. Each of these places experiences hot, dry summers and cool, wet winters. That's an unusual climatic combination, and one that puts a big demand on the region's plant and animal communities. All of them have to find a way to endure blazing sun and near drought conditions for some parts of the year, followed by months of intense rains and little sun.

Here in North America, Mediterranean conditions prevail over a lengthy section of the Pacific coast—from the redwood forests of northern California to the shrubby chaparral hillsides of the central coast to the coastal sage scrublands of southern California and the Baja Peninsula. We've included western Baja in this ecoregion because it has so much in common with the habitats to the north. Our term "California Coast" thus encompasses both the U.S. state of California and the Mexican states of Baja California and Baja California Sur. Although the central valley of California also experiences a Mediterranean climate, most of the valley lies in our Western Deserts and Plateaus ecoregion.

Of course, climate is not the only factor that has shaped the California Coast ecoregion. Waves have chipped away at the coastline, leaving cliffs and arches and other dramatic features along the water's edge. The California current, which infuses offshore waters with a cold arctic blast, helps produce the fog that regularly blankets the northern coast. Earthquakes have shaken the land and the lives of California's residents. Periodic wildfires have raged through the region, spurring plant growth but sometimes devastating human communities.

The California Coast ecoregion has also been profoundly shaped by its human inhabitants. American Indians actively managed the land for thousands of years by setting fires, harvesting acorns and grasses, and hunting game. Since then, Spanish missionaries, goldseekers, fameseekers, and a diverse assortment of people from all over the world have come to define and be defined by this striking coastal landscape.

Habitats

The land and waters along California's coast comprise a diversity of *habitats*—places where an organism finds the food, shelter, and space it needs to survive. Living within these habitats are a plethora of plant and animal species you won't find if you travel just a little farther inland and away from the Mediterranean influence. Santa Cruz kangaroo rats, Sonoma chipmunks, San Diego horned lizards, and California gnatcatchers are just a few of the creatures that live here and nowhere else in the world. That's part of what makes the California Coast such a special place. But it's also why conservationists are working so hard to protect it. With such a restricted range, many species can't survive the competition for space and resources from the human populations that love these Mediterranean places too.

Listed below are some of the major habitats you can find within this coastal region.

Rocky Shore: Along many stretches of the California coast, the waves of the Pacific crash not against soft, sandy beaches, but against rocks. These rocky shore habitats harbor a surprising amount of life. Giant green anemones and red tube worms sway in the tide pools that form in rocky depressions. Sea lions and harbor seals haul out on and around the rocks to rest and raise their young. Black oystercatchers and other shorebirds pick their way along the rocks feeding on limpets and other rock-clinging invertebrates.

If you see a rock face exposed at low tide, you'll notice that many of the resident invertebrates are organized vertically according to their relative tolerance for sun and water. Highest on the rocks are rock lice and other denizens of the *splash zone,* which seldom receive more than a

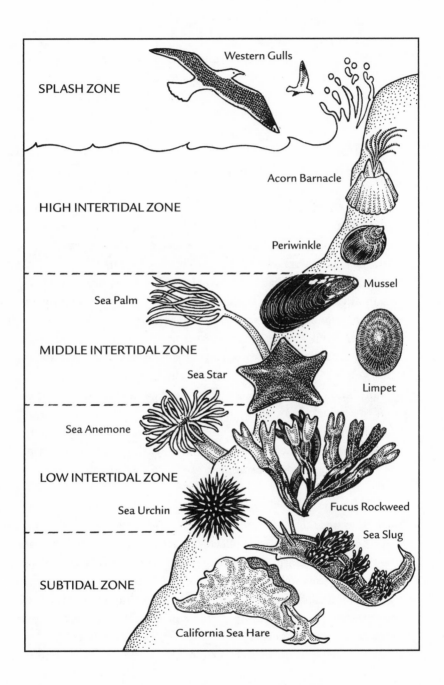

SPLASH ZONE

Western Gulls

HIGH INTERTIDAL ZONE

Acorn Barnacle

Periwinkle

Mussel

Sea Palm

MIDDLE INTERTIDAL ZONE

Sea Star

Limpet

Sea Anemone

LOW INTERTIDAL ZONE

Sea Urchin

Fucus Rockweed

Sea Slug

SUBTIDAL ZONE

California Sea Hare

moistening mist from the waves below. Farther below, acorn barnacles and periwinkles crowd the *high intertidal zone,* submerged only during the high tides. Sea stars, limpets, and sea palms cling to the rocks of the *middle intertidal zone,* employing super suction techniques to withstand the pounding waves. Sea urchins, anemones, sea grass, and other organisms stick to the *low intertidal zone,* which is only exposed during the lowest tides. And in the *subtidal zone* live rocky shore creatures that can never be exposed to the air, including nudibranches, California sea hares, and red abalones. (Examples: "The Long Bike Ride"; "Mysteries.")

Sea Cliffs: Walking along some of the more northern sections of the California coast, you'll see rugged sea cliffs made of granite, basalt, and other strong rocks left behind after the waves weathered away the softer rocks. Sea cliffs attract all sorts of seabirds who can roost among the high rocks with little fear of predators. Black oystercatchers and pelagic cormorants nest on steep ledges in the splash zone. Pigeon guillemots crowd the higher ledges—some of them so narrow that the birds can't even turn around and face the water when they're ready to fly off! Brandt's cormorants, the most common cormorants of the California Coast, choose gentler slopes on the cliffs. And double-crested cormorants and puffins lay their eggs in burrows near the top of the cliff.

If you're lucky enough to come across a sea cliff filled with nesting birds, experts recommend watching from a distance with a good pair of binoculars. Even a careful cliffwalker can unwittingly disrupt the birds or crush their fragile eggs. (Examples: "At Sea Ranch Beach"; "Swimming Lessons.")

Sandy Beach and Dune: When California's sandy beaches are crowded with joggers and sunbathers and volleyball players, it's easy to forget that an entire wildlife community lives here too. Find a quieter stretch of sand, and you might see herring gulls scavenging the high tide line for beached fish and mollusks. Small flocks of sanderlings race up and down with the waves, dipping for floating particles of food. Whimbrels and willets pluck razor clams and other burrowing critters out of the sand.

Hike up and away from the water, and you'll soon reach the sand dunes that form above the beach. Here the bare dune is occasionally speckled with the pink of beach morning glory, the white of seaside angelica, and the yellow hues of beach evening primrose. The roots of these and other dune plants help anchor the sand in place. (Examples: "Night Beach"; "To Catch a Grunion.")

Channel Islands: According to Chumash legend, California's Channel Islands were once the stomping grounds of giant humans more than forty feet tall. Nowadays, these eight islands, located twenty-five miles off the coast, are best known as a sanctuary for many of California's marine species. Northern elephant seals, northern sea lions, and 90 percent of the population of southern California sea lions breed on the rocky shores of San Nicolas and San Miguel Islands. Most of California's brown pelicans nest among the rocks of Anacapa Island. And of course, much of the region's life can be found in offshore waters. Giant kelp beds off Santa Rosa Island attract great schools of fish. Bottle-nosed dolphins, whales, and sharks can all be seen swimming in the vicinity of these islands at certain times of year.

Because the Channel Islands have been isolated from the mainland for so long, more than a hundred species of plants and animals have evolved here that exist nowhere else on Earth. These species are extremely vulnerable to competition from non-native plants and animals that have been introduced to the islands either intentionally or accidentally. Visit the Channel Islands and you may see the world's only island night lizards resting in the shade of rocks or spy island gray foxes bounding through the grasslands and even climbing trees! (Examples: "Catalina's Pigeon Express"; "The Lone Woman of San Nicolas Island"; "The Dolphins.")

Redwood Forest: For thousands of years, when North America was a wetter and warmer place, redwood trees covered a broad band of the continent. Today their descendants live only in a few places along the California coast where temperatures are still mild, the soil is moist, the humidity is high, and the desiccating effects of the sea air aren't too pronounced. Redwood trees can soar up to heights of three hundred feet—surpassing the Statue of Liberty. Their crowns are so high, in fact, that they are regularly shrouded by the fog clouds that roll in off the ocean. And that's key to their survival. The moisture in the clouds condenses on the redwoods' needles and drips to the ground, adding as much as twelve extra inches of water each year. This steady water supply makes up for the fact that the roots of the redwoods aren't equipped to absorb moisture from deep reservoirs.

Like a busy apartment building, a redwood buzzes with life from top to bottom. Western flycatchers, Steller's jays, and chestnut-backed chickadees flit around the canopy, snapping up insects from the air, bark, and leaves. Pygmy nuthatches and pileated woodpeckers probe the trunks in search of insects. Blue grouse nibble on nuts and berries on the ground, which is often covered with a dense mat of ferns and moss. Banana slugs slog through the moist duff, salamanders hide under leaves and in logs, and Sonoma and Townsends' chipmunks dart in and out of their underground tunnels. (Examples: "Camping Out in Redwood Country"; "In Trees.")

Oak Woodlands: In California's oak woodlands, life revolves around the humble acorn. Acorns are the fruits of the many oaks that, along with gray pines, dominate these open hilly habitats. They're also the most important food source for many woodland creatures. In fact, some oak woodland inhabitants have developed wily strategies for ensuring a steady acorn supply. Squirrels bury them in the soil. Dusky-footed woodrats stockpile them in their dens. Chipmunks drag them into their underground tunnels. Western scrub jays cache them in the ground. Acorn woodpeckers drill holes into dead trees and plug them with a snugly fitting acorn. As the acorns dry and shrink, woodpecker guardians move them to smaller holes so they won't fall out and be lost! Why all this attention to one small nut? Acorns are loaded with calories, giving animals a lot of energy for relatively little work. If carefully stowed, they can provide nutritious meals well through the winter months.

California's oak woodlands are becoming increasingly rare these days. Replaced by vineyards and residential areas, the woodlands were also removed for many years by land managers hoping to increase the productivity of their rangelands. Nowadays, people better recognize the value of oaks, but unfortunately, two diseases—oak wilt and sudden oak death syndrome—are hitting these trees with a vengeance. (Examples: "Coyote and the Acorns"; "A-Birding on a Bronco.")

Chaparral: Up and down the California Coast lie hills covered with large shrubby plants, such as toyon, chamise, manzanita, scrub oak, and ceanothus. This is California's chaparral habitat. Where the shrubs grow close together, chaparral can seem impenetrable to humans. But it makes a perfect cover for brush rabbits, which forge mazelike paths through the undergrowth, and for the sage sparrows, wrentits, and other birds that feed and nest within the shrubs.

Most chaparral shrubs are hardy evergreens, with waxy or needlelike leaves designed to hold in moisture during the hot, dry summer months. And all are adapted in some way to fires, which clear out the underbrush and boost the soil with nutrient-rich ash. Some chaparral species are downright fire dependent: Ione manzanita seeds germinate only after a fire, and mariposa lilies and fire poppies don't bloom until a fire has scorched the ground they grow on. (Examples: "Fire in the Chaparral!"; "Left Sink.")

Coastal Scrub: Horned lizards, cacti, and kangaroo rats give some parts of the California Coast a desertlike character. But in truth, these areas are coastal scrub—a habitat dominated by California sagebrush, California buckwheat, black sage, and prickly pear in the southern parts of this ecoregion, with bush monkeyflowers, sword ferns, and lemonade berry in the slightly wetter regions of the north.

Coastal scrub bears a close resemblance to chaparral. The plants are shrubby and fire-adapted. But they're even smaller, putting more of their growth safely underground. And they're even more drought-tolerant. Most plants do their growing during the cool, wet winters, and many of them shed their leaves during the summer to avoid drying out in the hot sun.

A number of rare animals inhabit California's coastal scrub lands, including orange-throated whiptails, coast horned lizards, California gnatcatchers, Costa's hummingbirds, San Diego pocket mice, and San Diego banded geckos. (Example: "Vasquez Rocks.")

Salt Marshes: Few people living around the San Francisco Bay probably know that it contains the largest salt marsh in the state. Packed with mollusks, crustaceans, and other small creatures, this habitat nourishes millions of migrating birds as they journey up and down the Pacific Flyway. Like other salt marshes, it provides a nursery ground for young fish and helps purify the waters of the bay. Unfortunately, the San Francisco Bay is one of the most invaded habitats in the world too, filled with marine creatures from all over the world that have reached the bay on ships and are now out-competing native species for food and living space.

You'll find salt marshes up and down the California coast, often at the juncture of river and sea. Eelgrass, cordgrass, and pickleweed dominate the vegetation. Avocets, stilts, snowy plovers, marbled godwits, and many other shorebirds peruse the mud flats for their favored foods. Salt-marsh harvest mice nibble on the pickleweed, scurrying to higher ground when the high tides come in. Even harbor seals sometimes visit the salt marsh to feed or raise their young. (Example: "The Marsh at the Edge of Arcata.")

Animals and Plants

It would take a whole book to describe the animals and plants of the California Coast. So we've simply listed below the organisms mentioned in this anthology and given a brief explanation, where necessary, of what they are.

Osprey

Birds: Birds can be grouped into several large categories, which may help to keep them straight. Mallards are *swimming birds.* Herring gulls, double-crested cormorants, pelagic cormorants (once known as violet-green cormorants), and brown pelicans are seabirds known as *aerialists.* *Long-legged wading birds* include great blue herons, black-crowned night herons, snowy egrets, and other egrets. Sandpipers, snipes, and dunlins are *smaller wading birds.* Osprey, red-tailed hawks, owls, white-tailed kites, and California condors are all *birds of prey.* California quails and mountain quails are *fowl-like birds.* Hummingbirds, Nuttall's woodpeckers, and other woodpeckers are all *non-perching land birds.* And among the many *perching land birds* are marsh wrens, crows, sage sparrows, ravens, finches, golden-crowned sparrows, towhees (also known as chewinks), warblers, vireos, lazuli buntings, western scrub jays, California thrashers, flycatchers, and wrentits.

Quail

Mammals: Sea lions, harbor seals, sea otters, dolphins, and whales are all marine mammals of the California Coast ecoregion. Land mammals include mountain lions, mule deer and black-tailed deer, coyotes, red fox, gray fox, opossums, raccoons, jackrabbits, cottontail rabbits, ground squirrels, western gray squirrels, pocket gophers, chipmunks, moles, and mice. Grizzly bears once roamed over large sections of the California Coast but have not been seen anywhere in the state since 1924.

Sea Lion

Harbor Seal

Marine Invertebrates: Marine invertebrates are sea creatures that don't have a backbone. You can group them in the following way. *Cnidarians* include jellyfish, corals, and sea anemones. *Mollusks* include abalones, mussels, octopuses, and sea snails. Hermit crabs, lobsters, barnacles, and ghost shrimp are all *arthropods.* Starfish, or sea stars, and sea urchins are spiny-skinned *echinoderms.* And most sea worms fall into the category of wormlike animals.

Sea Urchin

California Sister Butterfly

Terrestrial Invertebrates: Moths, butterflies, ants, damselflies, grasshoppers, and horseflies are *insects.* Spiders are *arachnids.*

Reptiles and Amphibians: Lizards and rattlesnakes are two of the many *reptiles* of the California Coast ecoregion. Like other reptiles, they have dry and scaly skin, and they lay their eggs on land. Pacific treefrogs and salamanders are *amphibians.* Clawless with moist skin, they lay their eggs in the water, and their young go through a change called metamorphosis as they develop into adulthood.

Whiptail Lizard

Fish: *Saltwater fish* include stingrays, herring, grunion, rockfish, salmon, smelt, and great white sharks (sharks are in a special group known as *cartilaginous fish*). Among the many *freshwater fish* of the region are steelhead trout.

Grunion

Plants: The *coniferous trees* of the California Coast ecoregion include redwoods, junipers, ponderosa pines, gray pines (formerly known as digger pines), hemlocks, and cypress trees. *Broadleaf trees and shrubs* include canyon live oak and other oaks, Pacific madrone, California laurel, maples, willows, California sycamore, eucalyptus, California buckeye, California hazelnut, plum trees, manzanitas, toyon, chamise, ceanothus, holly, sagebrush, evergreen huckleberry (which Mrs. J. B. Rideout calls "blueberry"), and rhododendrons. Broadly speaking, the following are *wildflowers:* cattail, fennel, cordgrass, pickleweed, bulrush, duckweed, clover, cheat grass, buckwheat, white sage, mint, mustard, prickly pear cactus, California lilac (or blue blossom), bougainvillea, lupine, poppies, monkeyflower, and forget-me-nots.

Toyon

Other: Mushrooms are a kind of *fungus.* Neither fungi, nor the group of organisms called *algae* are now considered part of the plant family. The algae of this ecoregion include feather boa kelp and other seaweeds.

Stories by Region

Parks and Preserves

Listed below are just a few of the many places where you can go to experience the wilder side of the California Coast ecoregion. Please note that the phone numbers provided are sometimes for the park's headquarters, but often for a managing agency or organization. In any case, the people at these numbers can provide you with details about the area and directions for how to get there!

Northern Coast

Angel Island State Park (Tiburon) 415-435-1915

Bolinas Lagoon Preserve of Audubon Canyon Ranch (Bolinas) 415-868-9244

Clear Lake State Park (Kelseyville) 707-279-4293

Farallon Islands National Wildlife Refuge (visitors are not allowed, but one can view the nesting seabirds and marine mammals via boat) 510-792-0222

Golden Gate National Recreation Area (San Francisco) 415-556-0560

Humboldt Bay National Wildlife Refuge (Loleta) 707-733-5406

Humboldt Lagoons State Park (Orick) 707-488-2041

Humboldt Redwoods State Park (Weott) 707-946-2409

Jug Handle State Reserve (Mendocino) 707-895-3141

King Range National Conservation Area (Shelter Cove) 707-825-2300

Lake Earl State Park (Crescent City) 707-464-6101, ext. 5112

MacKerricher State Park (Fort Bragg) 707-964-9112

Mendocino Headlands State Park (Mendocino) 707-937-5804

Mount Tamalpais State Park (Mill Valley) 415-388-2070

Muir Woods National Monument (Mill Valley) 415-388-2595

Patrick's Point State Park (Trinidad) 707-677-3570

Point Reyes National Seashore (Point Reyes Station) 415-464-5100

Redwood National and State Parks (Crescent City) 707-464-6101

Sinkyone Wilderness State Park (Whitethorn) 707-986-7711

Six Rivers National Forest (Eureka) 707-442-1721

Tomales Bay State Park (Inverness) 415-669-1140

Central Coast

Año Nuevo State Reserve (Pescadero) 650-879-0227

Big Basin Redwoods State Park (Boulder Creek) 831-338-8860

Robert W. Crown Memorial State Beach and Crab Cove Marine Reserve (Alameda) 510-562-7275

Don Edwards San Francisco Bay National Wildlife Refuge (Fremont) 510-792-0222

Elkhorn Slough National Estuarine Research Reserve (Watsonville) 831-728-2822

James V. Fitzgerald Marine Reserve (Moss Beach) 650-728-3584

Grizzly Island Wildlife Area/Suisun Marsh Complex (Suisun City) 707-425-3828

Guadalupe-Nipomo Dunes Preserve (Guadalupe) 805-343-2455

Montaña de Oro State Park (Morro Bay) 805-528-0513

Monterey Bay National Marine Sanctuary (Monterey) 831-647-4201

Morro Bay State Park (Morro Bay) 805-772-2560

Mount Diablo State Park (Clayton) 925-837-2525

Palo Alto Baylands Nature Reserve (Palo Alto) 650-329-2506

Pfeiffer Big Sur State Park (Big Sur) 831-667-2315

Pinnacles National Monument (Pinnacles) 831-389-4485

Point Lobos State Reserve (Carmel) 831-624-4909

Salinas River National Wildlife Refuge (Monterey) 510-792-0222

San Bruno Mountain State Park (Brisbane) 650-363-4020

San Pablo Bay National Wildlife Refuge (Vallejo) 707-562-3000

San Simeon State Park (San Simeon) 805-927-2020

Tilden Regional Park (Berkeley) 510-562-7275

Wilder Ranch State Park (Santa Cruz) 831-423-9703

Southern Coast

Angeles National Forest (Arcadia) 626-574-5200

Bolsa Chica State Beach and Ecological Reserve (Huntington Beach) 714-846-3460

Cabrillo National Monument (San Diego) 619-557-5450

Channel Islands National Park (Ventura) 805-658-5730

Cleveland National Forest (Alpine) 619-445-6235

Crystal Cove State Park (Laguna Beach) 949-494-3539

Cuyamaca Rancho State Park (Descanso) 760-765-0755

Devil's Punchbowl County Park (Pearblossom) 805-944-2743

Los Padres National Forest (Goleta) 805-968-6640

Malibu Creek State Park (Malibu) 818-880-0367

Malibu Lagoon State Beach (Malibu) 818-880-0350

McGrath State Beach (Ventura) 805-654-4744

Mount San Jacinto State Park and State Wilderness (Idyllwild) 909-659-2607

Palomar Mountain State Park (Palomar Mountain) 760-742-3462

Placerita Canyon Nature Center (Newhall) 661-259-7721

Point Mugu State Park (Oxnard) 818-880-0350

San Bernardino National Forest (San Bernardino) 909-383-5588

San Jacinto Wildlife Area (Lakeview) 909-654-0580

Santa Rosa Plateau Ecological Reserve (Lake Elsinore) 909-677-6951

Tijuana River National Estuarine Research Reserve (Imperial Beach) 619-575-3613

Topanga State Park (Topanga) 310-454-8212

Torrey Pines State Beach and State Reserve (Del Mar) 858-755-2063

Upper Newport Bay Ecological Reserve and Regional Park (Newport Beach) 949-640-6746

Vasquez Rocks Natural Area Park (Agua Dulce) 805-268-0840

Whittier Narrows Nature Center (South El Monte) 626-575-5523

Baja California

These parks are open to the public, but most of them do not have informational hotlines.

Constitución de 1857 National Park (near Ojos Negros)

El Vizcaíno Biosphere Reserve (Vizcaíno region)
Parque Natural de la Ballena Gris (Laguna Ojo de Liebra)
Sierra de San Pedro Mártir National Park (near San Telmo)
Sierra de la Laguna (near Miraflores)

Recommended Reading

Alden, Peter, et al. *National Audubon Society Field Guide to California.* New York: Alfred A. Knopf, 1998.

Bakker, Elna S. *An Island Called California: An Ecological Introduction to Its Natural Communities.* Berkeley: University of California Press, 1984.

Buckley, Christopher and Gary Young, eds. *The Geography of Home: California's Poetry of Place.* Berkeley: Heyday Books, 1999.

Gilbar, Steven. *Natural State: A Literary Anthology of California Nature Writing.* Berkeley: University of California Press, 1998.

Hickman, Pamela. *At the Seashore: Pacific Edition.* Halifax, Nova Scotia: Formac Publishing Company, 1997.

Johnston, Verna. *California Forests and Woodlands: A Natural History.* Berkeley: University of California Press, 1994.

McConnaughey, Bayard H. and Evelyn McConnaughey. *Pacific Coast.* (Audubon Society Nature Guides.) New York: Alfred A. Knopf, 1985.

Niesen, Thomas M. *Beachcomber's Guide to California Marine Life.* Houston: Gulf Publishing Company, 1994.

Special Thanks

Many people have contributed hours of hard work and copious creativity to this anthology, most notably the staff of Milkweed Editions and the authors whose work is presented in these pages. My own work as editor has benefited every step of the way from the support of friends, family, and colleagues.

My sister, Claire Mercurio, helped launch me on my California literary journey by sending me a book of Chumash stories from her home region more than a year ago. I hope this anthology adds to the pleasure and effectiveness of her wonderful work with young people.

Miriam Stewart kindly joined me for a day of poetry reading, once again demonstrating her ability to limn the strengths and weaknesses of a poem in a moment's time. Robin Kelsey displayed heroic generosity by putting aside his dissertation on many occasions to read a selection or answer a perplexing question.

Jen Kretser, Priscilla Howell, and Jen Lindstrom took time out from their busy schedules to read and respond to the entire draft manuscript. As usual, their comments reflected their great sensitivity to young people, literature, and the natural world.

Megan Amundson volunteered considerable time to assist me with research and Spanish translation. I'm grateful for her help and for her unflagging patience.

Martha Hoopes, a fellow graduate of Williams and now a postdoctoral fellow in the department of integrative biology at the University of California at Berkeley, reviewed the introduction and appendixes with a blessedly critical eye. Any errors that remain are entirely my own.

In the process of creating this anthology, I worked to finalize our complete map of North American ecoregions. Gary Paul Nabhan sketched out the original configuration of ecoregions, and then dozens of colleagues reviewed it and offered suggestions. While taking responsibility for any final choices that differ from their own, I offer my heartfelt thanks to Martha Hoopes, Jen Kretser, Tim Farnham, Paul Jahnige, Beth Olson, April Pulley Sayre, Jeremy Wilson, Luise Woelflein, and Tim Wohlgenant.

Finally, I wish to extend my gratitude to my parents, Lloyd and Ted St. Antoine, who have nurtured and supported me in just about every way imaginable throughout my lifetime. This year, they made it possible for me to visit the California Coast in the midst of working on this anthology. I will always relish the memories of our California family reunion, and will never forget walking under the giant redwoods watching Michael, Mary, Paul, and Max chase each other in and out of the leafy shadows.

Contributor Acknowledgments

Ellery Akers, "Left Sink," in *Intimate Nature: The Bond Between Women and Animals,* ed. Linda Hogan, Deena Metzger, and Brenda Peterson. (New York: Ballantine Books, 1998), 245–49. Copyright © 1990 by Ellery Akers. Reprinted with permission from the author. First published in *Sierra* 75, no. 6 (November/December 1990).

Sue Alexander, "Vasquez Rocks." Copyright © 2001 by Sue Alexander. Printed with permission from Curtis Brown, Ltd.

Virginia Barrett, "Fog—San Francisco." Copyright © 2001 by Virginia Barrett. Printed with permission from the author.

Richard Bauman, "Catalina's Pigeon Express," *Cricket* 25, no. 11 (July 1998): 45–48. Copyright © 1998 by Richard Bauman. Reprinted with permission from *Cricket* magazine.

Robin Beeman, "In Trees." Copyright © 2001 by Robin Beeman. Printed with permission from the author.

Mélina Brown, "The Long Bike Ride." Copyright © 2001 by Mélina Brown. Printed with permission from the author.

Roberto Castillo Udiarte, "Entomológica," in *Un Camino de Hallazgos: Poetas Bajacalifornianos del Siglo Veinte,* ed. Gabriel Trujillo Muñoz (Colonia Nueva, Mexico: Universidad Autónoma de Baja California, 1992), 81–82. Copyright © 1992 by Roberto Castillo Udiarte. Reprinted with permission from the author. English trans. Megan Amundson and Anne Edstrom.

J. Smeaton Chase, "Quicksand on the Gaviota Coast," excerpted from *Natural State: A Literary Anthology of California Nature Writing,* ed. Steven Gilbar (Berkeley: University of California Press, 1998), 237–39. First published in *California Coast Trails: A Horseback Ride from Mexico to Oregon* (Boston: Houghton Mifflin, 1913).

Vic Coccimiglio, "Night Beach," in *The Invisible Ladder,* ed. Liz Rosenberg. (New York: Henry Holt, 1996), 35. Copyright © 1996 by Vic Coccimiglio. Reprinted with permission from the author.

Olga Cossi, "There Oughter Be an Otter!" Copyright © 2001 by Olga Cossi. Printed with permission from the author.

"Coyote and the Acorns," traditional Yurok story in *The Way We Lived: California Indian Reminiscences, Stories, and Songs,* ed. Malcolm Margolin (Berkeley: Heyday Books, 1981), 139–40. First published in Jean Sapir, "Yurok Tales" *Journal of American Folklore* 41 (1928): 254. The story was narrated by a Yurok woman named Mrs. Haydom in the summer of 1927.

Nancy Dawson, "Seacoast Secret." Copyright © 2001 by Nancy Dawson. Printed with permission from the author.

Danielle Jeanne Drolet, "The Marsh at the Edge of Arcata." Copyright © 2001 by Danielle Jeanne Drolet. Printed with permission from the author.

Daniel Duane, "Surfing with Sharks," excerpted from chapter seven of *Caught Inside: A Surfer's Year on the California Coast* (New York: North Point Press, 1996), 59–66. Copyright © 1996 by Daniel Duane. Reprinted with permission from North Point Press, a division of Farrar, Straus and Giroux, LLC.

"The Earth Dragon," in *American Indian Myths and Legends,* ed. Richard Erdoes and Alfonso Ortiz (New York: Pantheon Books, 1984), 107–9. Copyright © 1984 by Richard Erdoes and Alfonso Ortiz. Reprinted with permission from Pantheon Books, a division of Random House, Inc.

Manuel Figuroa, "Pacific Coast Storm." Copyright © 2001 by Manuel Figuroa. Printed with permission from the author.

Marian Haddad, "Dark Sky," *San Diego Writer's Monthly* 9, no. 4 (May/June 1999): 8. Copyright © 1999 by Marian Haddad. Reprinted with permission from the author.

Dan Harder, "The Poppy," *Witness* 9, no. 1 (1995): 17. Copyright © 1995 by Dan Harder. Reprinted with permission from the author.

Jeffrey Harrison, "Swimming Lessons," in *The Singing Underneath* (New York: E. P. Dutton, 1988), 52. Copyright © 1988 by Jeffrey Harrison. Reprinted with permission from the author.

Aileen Kilgore Henderson, "To Catch a Grunion." Copyright © 2001 by Aileen Kilgore Henderson. Printed with permission from the author.

Jane Hirshfield, "Invocation" in *Of Gravity and Angels* (Middletown, Conn.: Wesleyan University Press, 1988). Copyright © 1988 by Jane Hirshfield. Reprinted with permission from University Press of New England.

Marlon K. Hom, trans., "In the New Garden," published as #123 in *Songs of Gold Mountain: Cantonese Rhymes from San Francisco Chinatown* (Berkeley: University of California Press, 1987), 211. Copyright © 1987 by the Regents of the University of California. Reprinted with permission from the Regents of the University of California and University of California Press.

Kathryn Hulme, "Earthquake and Fire," excerpted from *We Lived As Children* (New York: Alfred A. Knopf, 1938), 64–71, 74–76, 79–87. Copyright © 1938 by Kathryn Hulme. Copyright renewed © 1966 by Kathryn Hulme. Reprinted with permission from Brandt and Hochman Literary Agents, Inc.

Christina Hutchins, "Napa during El Niño." Copyright © 2001 by Christina Hutchins. Printed with permission from the author.

Helen Foster James, "The Lone Woman of San Nicolas Island." Copyright © 2001 by Helen Foster James. Printed with permission from the author.

Cherylene Lee, "Hollywood and the Pits," in *American Dragons,* ed. Laurence Yep (New York: HarperCollins, 1993), 34–47. Copyright © 1993 by Cherylene Lee. Reprinted with permission from Bret Adams, Ltd.

Florence A. Merriam, "A-Birding on a Bronco," excerpted from *A-Birding on a Bronco* (Boston: Houghton Mifflin, 1896), 1–7, 19.

David Meuel, "The Dolphins." Copyright © 2001 by David Meuel. Printed with permission from the author.

Mitali Perkins, "The Lost Hills." Copyright © 2001 by Mitali Perkins. Printed with permission from the author.

Mrs. J. B. Rideout, "Camping Out in Redwood Country," excerpted from *Camping Out in California* (San Francisco: R. R. Patterson, 1889), 5–6, 11–16, 22–24, 27–29, 33–38, 41–42, 49–50.

William Pitt Root, "Ode to a Plain Old Pond Frog." Copyright © 2001 by William Pitt Root. Printed with permission from the author.

Alison Seevak, "Plum Trees," in *What Have You Lost?* ed. Naomi Shibab Nye (New York: Greenwillow Books, 1999), 118. Copyright © 1999 by Alison Seevak. Reprinted with permission from the author.

Felicia Silcox, "The Secret of C. D. Parkhurst." Copyright © 2001 by Felicia Silcox. Printed with permission from the author.

Gary Snyder, "The Real Work," in *Turtle Island* (New York: New Directions, 1974), 32. Copyright © 1974 by Gary Snyder. Reprinted with permission from New Directions Publishing Corp.

Gabriel Trujillo Muñoz, "Aparición," in *A Plena Luz* (San Angel, Mexico: Consejo Nacional para la Cultura y las Artes, 1992), 87. Copyright © 1992 by Consejo Nacional para la Cultura y las Artes. Reprinted with permission from the author. "Apparition," in *Permanent Work: Poems 1981–1992,* trans. Patricia L. Irby, Robert L. Jones, and Gustavo V. Segade with the

About the Editor

Sara St. Antoine grew up in Ann Arbor, Michigan. She holds a bachelor's degree in English from Williams College, and a master's degree in Environmental Studies from the Yale School of Forestry and Environmental Studies. Currently living in Cambridge, Massachusetts, she enjoys walking along the Charles River and seeing black-crowned night herons hunkered in the trees.

About the Illustrators

Paul Mirocha is a designer and illustrator of books about nature for children and adults. His first book, *Gathering the Desert,* by Gary Paul Nabhan, won the 1985 John Burroughs Medal for natural history. He lives in Tucson, Arizona, with his daughters, Anna and Claire.

Trudy Nicholson is an illustrator of nature with a background in medical and scientific illustration. She received her B.S. in Fine Arts at Columbia University and has worked as a natural-science illustrator in a variety of scientific fields for many years. She lives in Cabin John, Maryland.

The World As Home, the nonfiction publishing program of Milkweed Editions, is dedicated to exploring our relationship to the natural world. Not espousing any particular environmentalist or political agenda, these books are a forum for distinctive literary writing that not only alerts the reader to vital issues but offers personal testimonies to living harmoniously with other species in urban, rural, and wilderness communities.

Milkweed Editions publishes with the intention of making a humane impact on society, in the belief that literature is a transformative art uniquely able to convey the essential experiences of the human heart and spirit. To that end, Milkweed publishes distinctive voices of literary merit in handsomely designed, visually dynamic books, exploring the ethical, cultural, and esthetic issues that free societies need continually to address. Milkweed Editions is a not-for-profit press.

For more information on other books published by Milkweed Editions for intermediate readers, contact Milkweed at (800) 520-6455 or visit our website (www.milkweed.org).

Books for Middle-Grade Readers
by Milkweed Editions

Tides by V. M. Caldwell

The Ocean Within by V. M. Caldwell

The Monkey Thief by Aileen Kilgore Henderson

Treasure of Panther Peak by Aileen Kilgore Henderson

The Dog with Golden Eyes by Frances Wilbur

Join Us

Milkweed publishes adult and children's fiction, poetry, and, in its World As Home program, literary nonfiction about the natural world. Milkweed also hosts two websites: www.milkweed.org, where readers can find in-depth information about Milkweed books, authors, and programs, and www.worldashome.org, which is your online resource of books, organizations, and writings that explore ethical, esthetic, and cultural dimensions of our relationship to the natural world. Since its genesis as *Milkweed Chronicle* in 1979, Milkweed has helped hundreds of emerging writers reach their readers. Thanks to the generosity of foundations and of individuals like you, Milkweed Editions is able to continue its nonprofit mission of publishing books chosen on the basis of literary merit—of how they impact the human heart and spirit—rather than on how they impact the bottom line. That's a miracle that our readers have made possible.

In addition to purchasing Milkweed books, you can join the growing community of Milkweed supporters. Individual contributions of any amount are both meaningful and welcome. Contact us for a Milkweed catalog or log on to www.milkweed.org and click on "About Milkweed," then "Why Join Milkweed," to find out about our donor program, or simply call (800) 520-6455 and ask about becoming one of Milkweed's contributors. As a nonprofit press, Milkweed belongs to you, the community. Milkweed's board, its staff, and especially the authors whose careers you help launch thank you for reading our books and supporting our mission in any way you can.

Interior design by Wendy Holdman
The text is typeset in 12/16 point Legacy Book
by Stanton Publication Services, Inc.
Printed on acid-free, recycled 55# Frasier Miami Book paper
by Friesen Corporation

THE

NORTHWEST

PACIFIC

COAST

BOREAL

ROCKY MOUNTAINS

GREAT

NORT

CALIFORNIA

WESTERN

COAST

DESERTS

AND

PLATEAUS

HAWAIIAN

ISLANDS